Disclaimer

The publisher of this book is by no way associated with the National Institute of Standards and Technology (NIST). The NIST did not publish this book. It was published by 50 page publications under the public domain license.

50 Page Publications.

Book Title: A Model-Based Analysis of First-Generation Service Discovery Systems

Book Author: Christopher E. Dabrowski; Kevin L. Mills; Stephen Quirolgico

Book Abstract: Future commercial software systems will be based on distributed service-oriented architectures in which applications are composed dynamically from remote components. A key part of service-oriented computing is the ability for clients to discover remote services that fulfill specific requirements. Since the mid-1990s, various commercial and public domain designs for service discovery systems have been proposed that enable clients and services to rendezvous in a distributed system. The report characterizes such designs as first-generation service discovery systems, based on the belief that experience with these systems will lead to future, improved designs. Using three widely used service discovery systems as a basis, this publication first presents a high level overview of the operation of service discovery protocols. A detailed generic model of first-generation service discovery systems, written in UML, follows this. The UML model provides an in-depth analysis of the alternative service discovery designs available today, including the major functional components that comprise these designs, the behaviors of these components, and the information they exchange. The report verifies the generality of the model by mapping its component element to corresponding elements of existent and emerging service discovery systems. This report also identifies issues that designers should attempt to resolve in the next generation of service discovery systems. The analysis is then extended to provide designers of future service discovery systems with a means to evaluate designs. First, the report proposes a set of service goals that service discovery systems should strive to satisfy to ensure a desirable level of quality of service. These goals provide a basis to define metrics, for evaluation the behavior and measuring performance of system designs and implementations. Second, the report identifies potential performance issues that may arise during operation of service discovery systems. Identifying performance issues can alert designers and implementers to the potential for unexpected behavior when service discovery technology is deployed at large scale. The report presents possible solutions to performance problems that extend well-known optimization algorithms for distributed systems and present new algorithms tailored to service discovery environments. The contributions in this report will help to improve the quality of the next generation of service discovery systems on which the service-oriented architectures of tomorrow appear likely to depend. Further, should an industry standards group choose to develop a unified specification for service discovery, the model should provide helpful input to the process.

Citation: NIST SP - 500-260

Keyword: Networking

NIST Special Publication 500-260

A Model-based Analysis of First-Generation Service Discovery Systems

Christopher Dabrowski
Kevin L. Mills
Stephen Quirolgico

NIST National Institute of Standards and Technology • Technology Administration • U.S. Department of Commerce

NIST Special Publication 500-260

A Model-based Analysis of First-Generation Service Discovery Systems

Christopher Dabrowski
Kevin L. Mills
Stephen Quirolgico
Information Technology Laboratory

October 2005

U.S. Department of Commerce
Carlos M. Gutierrez, Secretary

Technology Administration
Phillip J. Bond, Under Secretary for Technology

National Institute of Standards and Technology
William A. Jeffrey, Director

National Institute of Standards and Technology Special Publication 500-260
Natl. Inst. Stand. Technol. Spec. Publ. 500-260, 110 pages (October 2005)
CODEN: NSPUE2

U.S. GOVERNMENT PRINTING OFFICE
WASHINGTON: 2005

For sale by the Superintendent of Documents, U.S. Government Printing Office
Internet: bookstore.gpo.gov — Phone: (202) 512-1800 — Fax: (202) 512-2250
Mail: Stop SSOP, Washington, DC 20402-0001

Acknowledgements

The authors wish to thank their many colleagues who contributed to the research, analysis, and experimentation leading up to this special publication. The foundation for this work began in 1999 when a small group of researchers at NIST met to share their individual analyses of specific service discovery systems proposed by industry. The initial group included Chris Dabrowski, Olivier Mathieu, Kevin Mills, Doug Montgomery, and Scott Rose. Over the duration of the research leading up to this publication a range of others contributed, including Kevin Bowers, Mackenzie Britton, Jesse Elder, Stephen Quirolgico, Andrew Rukhin, Vasughi Sundramoorthy, and Ceryen Tan. Without the many contributions from these dedicated and curious researchers, this publication would not exist. Thanks are also due to the many reviewers, both inside and outside of NIST, who provided helpful suggestions to improve the various ideas incorporated in this publication. We also must not ignore the significant contributions made by the designers, specification writers, and implementers who developed the proposed technologies for service discovery, which formed the basis for the analyses reported here. Without the imagination and resources of these industrial contributors, we would not be in a position to provide the knowledge we gained by studying the designs for various service discovery systems. A select few individuals who had the foresight to provide funding to support the research reported here provided a final, but key, contribution to this work. Funding was provided by: Susan Zevin, as acting director of the NIST Information Technology Laboratory, Douglas Maughan, as manager of the Defense Advanced Research Projects Agency (DARPA) Fault-Tolerant Networks Program, John Salasin, as manager of the DARPA program in Dynamic Assembly for System Adaptability, Dependability and Assurance, and James Puffenbarger of the Advanced Research and Development Activity (ARDA).

EXECUTIVE SUMMARY

Information technology is undergoing a paradigm shift from desktop computing, where isolated workstations connect to shared servers across a network, to pervasive computing, where myriad portable, embedded, and networked information appliances continuously reconfigure themselves individually and collectively to support the information requirements of mobile workers and work teams. This shift will not occur overnight, nor will it be achieved without solving a range of new technical and social problems. Still, this inexorable change should yield many economic opportunities for the global information technology industry, and for the increasing swath of businesses that depend on information. The potential value of pervasive computing motivated the NIST Information Technology Laboratory (ITL) to establish a five-year program of research to help the information technology industry identify and solve some looming technical roadblocks that seemed likely to slow development and acceptance of the new paradigm. The ITL Pervasive Computing program addressed three general areas: human-computer interaction, programming models, and networking. Service discovery systems, which reside in an intersection between programming models and networking, cover a key aspect of pervasive computing. For this reason, researchers in ITL decided to study various industry designs for service discovery systems that could play a key part in future technology to enable pervasive computing applications. This special publication provides an analysis of a first generation of designs for service discovery systems.

Over the period from about 1998 to 2000, industry developed a first generation of competing architectures and protocols for device and service discovery. Such a plethora of incompatible approaches might impede the interoperability required by a market for pervasive computing. Is the existence of so many different service discovery systems justified? NIST researchers analyzed various technical approaches and developed a model to unify the features, functions, and processes provided. The goal of this modeling effort was threefold: (1) to understand the essential service-discovery functionality provided by the industry, (2) to reveal any technical deficiencies in existing service-discovery specifications, and (3) to define the technical bounds achievable from this first-generation of service-discovery systems. The result of this modeling effort is reported in this special publication.

The fact that numerous competing designs have appeared indicates a substantial industry interest in using dynamic service discovery as a means to deploy and evolve component-based systems. But why have so many different designs appeared? Are the designs sufficiently different to warrant multiple solutions? What elements are contained within the various designs? What problems should service discovery systems solve? What are the shortcomings of the first-generation of service discovery systems? What open issues do first-generation designs for service discovery systems leave for implementers to solve? These are the questions that motivate the work reported in this publication.

Based on careful analyses of selected specifications for service discovery architectures and protocols, we present a generic model that represents the key elements, relationships, and behaviors of a service discovery system. Our model consists of two parts: a meta-model that defines the context in which service discovery systems operate and a generic, object-oriented model that represents the fundamental structure and behavior of service discovery systems. We also identify some open issues or limitations in existing designs for first-generation service discovery systems. We demonstrate how our generic model can be used to represent specific service discovery systems.

Beyond an analysis of the structure and behavior of first-generation service discovery systems, we consider two other problems. First, the current generation of service discovery systems can lead to some system-wide performance issues, unless implementers and users exercise due care. We identify three classes of performance issues that might arise, and we suggest a range of solutions that implementers might adopt to solve each issue. A second problem relates to service guarantees. None of the service discovery systems we analyzed defined any expectations about the guarantees, or even the goals, that the design aimed to satisfy. We propose a set of service guarantees that we believe service discovery systems should aim to achieve, and we explain the qualifications associated with such guarantees. In other work, we have used our proposed service guarantees to assess the performance and correctness of specific designs for service discovery systems.

In summary, this special publication makes three specific contributions – intended to inform a future generation of designs and to improve the performance of implementations for the current generation of designs. First, we provide a generic model of the structure and behavior of first-generation service discovery systems, and we show how our model can represent the designs for several, specific service discovery systems. Our model unifies the common elements and behaviors in modern service discovery systems. Should an industry standards group choose to develop a unified specification for service discovery, our model could provide helpful input to the process. We also identify issues that designers should attempt to resolve in the next generation of service discovery systems. Second, we propose a set of service guarantees that we believe service discovery systems should strive to satisfy, along with an analysis of the factors that might interfere with meeting service guarantees. Such service guarantees could be cast into test assertions that serve to evaluate the behavior or measure the performance of designs and implementations of service discovery systems. Third, we identify and suggest possible solutions to performance issues that can arise in dynamic service discovery systems. Identifying possible performance issues can alert users to the potential for unexpected behavior when service discovery technology is deployed at large scale. Further, implementers of service discovery systems can consider our suggested solutions when developing software to embody related processes in a service discovery system. Our three contributions should help to improve the quality of the next generation of service discovery systems on which the service-oriented architectures of tomorrow appear likely to depend.

A Model-based Analysis of First-Generation Service Discovery Systems

Table of Contents

A Model-based Analysis of First-Generation Service Discovery Systems

1. Introduction

Software systems are evolving toward a form where applications can be composed dynamically from distributed components. A key part of such a paradigm is the ability for clients to discover services that fulfill specific requirements. Over the past five or six years, various designs have been proposed for service discovery systems [1-11] that can help clients and services to rendezvous in a distributed system. We characterize such designs as *first-generation service discovery systems*, based on our belief that experience with these systems will lead to future, improved designs.

The fact that numerous competing designs have appeared indicates a substantial industry interest in using dynamic service discovery as a means to deploy and evolve component-based systems. But why have so many different designs appeared? Are the designs sufficiently different to warrant multiple solutions? What elements are contained within the various designs? What problems should service discovery systems solve? What are the shortcomings of the first-generation of service discovery systems? What open issues do first-generation designs for service discovery systems leave for implementers to solve? These are the questions that motivate the work reported in this paper.

A few previous papers [12-16] have compared various service discovery systems at a functional or programming level. In general, these previous comparisons exhibit some significant shortcomings. First, most extant comparisons fail to consider the deeper design issues underlying service discovery systems. Second, most comparisons discuss various designs using concepts and terminology adopted from the related specifications, which makes it difficult for readers to draw comparisons among similar or distinct ideas.

In this paper, we adopt a different approach to analyzing first-generation service discovery systems. Based on a careful analysis of some specifications [1,3,5] for service discovery architectures and protocols, we developed a generic model that represents the key elements, relationships, and behaviors of a service discovery system. Our model consists of two parts: a meta-model (see Section 2) that defines the context in which service discovery systems operate and a generic, object-oriented model (see Section 3) that represents the fundamental structure and behavior of service discovery systems. We also identify some open issues or limitations (Section 3.6) in existing designs for first-generation service discovery systems. In a later section (Section 6), we show how our generic model can be used to represent specific service discovery systems, including the three – Universal Plug-and-Play (UPnP), Jini, and the Service Location Protocol (SLP) – we analyzed in creating our model, but also including two service discovery systems – the Web Services Dynamic Discovery [9] and the Globus Monitoring and Discovery Service (MDS) [10] – that we did not analyze when creating our model.

Beyond an analysis of the structure and behavior of first-generation service discovery systems, we also consider two other problems. First, the current generation of service discovery systems can lead to some system-wide performance issues, unless implementers and users exercise due care. We identify (see Section 4) three classes of performance issues that might arise, and we suggest a range of solutions that implementers might adopt to solve each issue. A second problem relates to service guarantees. None of the service discovery systems we analyzed defined any expectations about the guarantees, or even the goals, that the design aimed to satisfy. We propose (see Section 5) a set of service guarantees that we believe service discovery systems should aim to achieve, and we explain the qualifications associated with such guarantees. In other work [17-21], we have used our proposed service guarantees to assess the performance and correctness of specific designs for service discovery systems.

We can summarize the contributions of this paper along several lines. First, we provide a generic model of the structure and behavior of first-generation service discovery systems, and we show how our model can represent the designs for several, specific service discovery systems. Our model provides a deep analysis of the common elements and behaviors in modern service discovery systems. Further, should an industry standards group choose to develop a unified specification for service discovery, our model should provide helpful input to the process. We also identify issues that designers should attempt to resolve in the next generation of service discovery systems. Second, we propose a set of service goals that we believe service discovery systems should strive to satisfy, along with an analysis of the factors that might interfere with meeting service goals. Such service goals could be cast into test assertions that serve to evaluate the behavior or measure the performance of designs and implementations of service discovery systems. Finally, we identify and suggest possible solutions to performance issues that can arise in dynamic service discovery systems. Identifying possible performance issues can alert users to the potential for unexpected behavior when service discovery technology is deployed at large scale. Further, implementers of service discovery systems can consider our suggested solutions when developing software to embody related processes in a service discovery system. All of our contributions can help to improve the quality of the next generation of service discovery systems on which the service-oriented architectures of tomorrow appear likely to depend.

2. Modeling First-Generation Service Discovery Architectures

In subsequent sections of this paper, we define a generic model that captures the fundamental structural and behavioral design choices embodied in many of the current, first-generation, service discovery systems. In this section, we present a rigorous architectural framework in which to ground our generic model. We begin with a general overview of service discovery systems, accompanied by a summary of selected first-generation service discovery systems, and then we become more formal.

2.1 Informal Description of Service Discovery Systems. Service discovery systems enable distributed components (i.e., software objects executing on different computer nodes in a network) to: (1) discover each other without prior arrangement, (2) describe opportunities for collaboration, (3) compose themselves into topologies that cooperate to meet application needs, and (4) detect and adapt to topology changes. To achieve these objectives, service discovery systems rely on architectures where distributed components exchange messages in accordance with behaviors defined by service discovery protocols. In the simplest service discovery system, a client might seek to discover a list of services (e.g., printers, calendars, mail servers, web servers) available on a network and display the list through a graphical-user interface (GUI); thus, this architecture consists of two parties: client and service. The service discovery protocol that supports such a two-party architecture (see Figure 2-1) might allow a client to send a query for any service to a network multicast group, where all services would be required to listen. Upon receiving a multicast query for any service, the protocol might require that a service send a description of itself directly to the client.

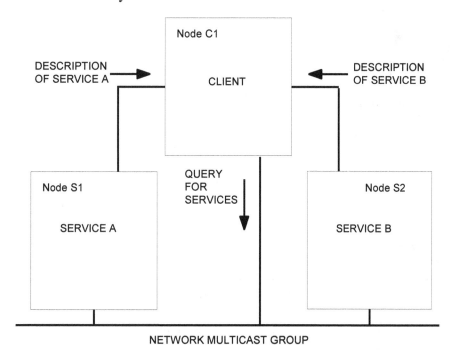

Figure 2-1. A Sample Two-Party Service Discovery Architecture with One Client and Two Services

In a more complex service discovery system, a client might seek to discover a set of
directories and then to query one of those directories to obtain a list of services known by
the directory; thus, this architecture consists of three parties: client, directory, and service.
The service discovery protocol that supports such a three-party architecture (see Figure 2-
2) might require a service to send a query for any directory to a network multicast group,
where every directory would be required to listen. In addition, directories might be
required to announce their presence periodically, which implies that directories might be
discovered either by listening for multicast directory announcements or by sending
multicast queries to directories.

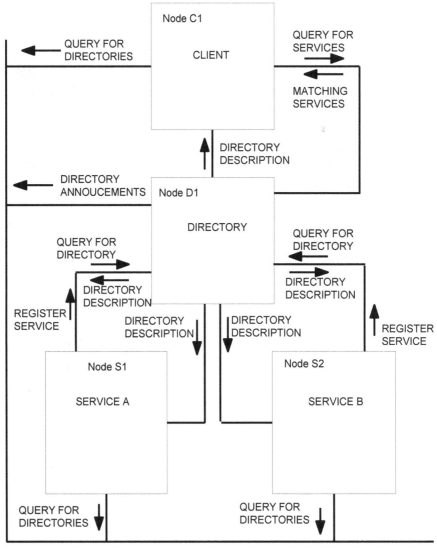

Figure 2-2. A Sample Three-Party Architecture with
One Client, One Directory, and Two Services

The supporting protocol might require that a client or service, after learning of a directory through a multicast announcement, query a directory directly to obtain a description of the directory. The protocol might also require that a directory, upon receiving a multicast query for any directory, send a description of itself directly to the querying client or service. The protocol might require the service, upon receiving a directory description, to send a description of itself directly to the directory. The protocol might allow a client that learns of a directory to send a query directly to the directory to request a list of the services known by the directory. The directory would likely be required to return a list of relevant services.

2.2 Overview of Selected First-Generation Service Discovery Systems. In what follows, we briefly describe a two-party (Universal-Plug-and-Play, or UPnP), three-party (Jini Networking Technology), and adaptive (Service-Location Protocol, or SLP) service discovery system. SLP operates as a three-party system, but adapts to a two-party system when necessary. As discussed later, the properties and behavior of these first-generation discovery systems will form the basis for a general service discovery model.

2.2.1 UPnP. UPnP defines an architecture that enables control points (clients) to discover root devices (which contain devices and services) without a directory. In UPnP, root devices are service containers, which may include a hierarchical set of subordinate devices and services; thus, one can view each root device as a top-level service that describes itself and its subordinate services. Upon startup, each control point (CP) and root device (RD) engages in a discovery process. In a lazy-discovery process, each RD periodically announces its services over a multicast group. Upon receiving these announcements, CPs with matching requirements use a HTTP/TCP (HyperText Transfer Protocol/transmission-control protocol) unicast link to request, directly from the RD, descriptions of relevant services. The CP stores copies of service descriptions in a local cache. Alternatively, the CP may engage in an aggressive-discovery process, where the CP transmits its service requirements as queries on a multicast group. Any RD containing a service with matching requirements may use a HTTP/UDP (user-datagram protocol) unicast link to respond (after a jitter delay) directly to the CP. For each device or service of interest, the CP uses a HTTP/TCP unicast link to request a copy of the relevant descriptions, caching them locally. To maintain a service description in its local cache, a CP expects to receive periodic announcements from the relevant RD, which announces the existence of service descriptions at a specified interval, known as a Time-to-Live, or TTL. Each announcement specifies the TTL value. If the CP does not receive an announcement from the RD within the TTL, then the CP may discard the discovered service description.

UPnP service descriptions may identify state variables that can be monitored on behalf of CPs. Interested CPs send a subscribe request, and the RD responds by either accepting the subscription, or denying the request. The subscription, if accepted, is retained for a TTL, which may be refreshed with subsequent subscribe requests from the CP. Whenever the state of a monitored variable changes, the monitor announces the change by sending events to all subscribed CPs.

2.2.2 Jini. Jini defines an architecture that enables clients and services to rendezvous through a third party, known as a *lookup service* (Jini terminology for a directory). Upon startup, a Jini component (client, service, or lookup service) engages in a discovery process to locate other, relevant Jini components within the network neighborhood. Jini encompasses two discovery modes, *multicast* and *unicast*, where multicast discovery is supported by two discovery processes, which we call aggressive and lazy. Upon initiation, a Jini component enters aggressive discovery by transmitting discovery messages (*probes*) at a fixed interval for a specified period, or until discovering a sufficient number of lookup services. Each probe contains a list of lookup services previously discovered in order to allow potential responders to suppress duplicate replies. Upon cessation of aggressive discovery, a component enters lazy discovery, listening for announcements sent at intervals by lookup services. Once a relevant lookup service is discovered, the discovering component requests an application-programming interface (API) that enables the component to interact with the lookup service.

Unicast discovery operates differently from multicast discovery. In unicast discovery, each Jini component may be given a specific list of lookup services to discover. For each lookup service on the list, a Jini component establishes a TCP connection and requests an API. Should the lookup service prove unavailable, the component can continue to retry connecting.

A Jini service registers a description of itself with each discovered lookup service. A Jini client may register a request to be notified by a lookup service of arriving or departing services of interest, or of changes in the attributes describing services of interest. A registering component (client or service) requests registration for a duration, which may be accepted for a granted lease period. To extend registration beyond the granted lease period, registering components must renew the lease before it expires; otherwise, registration is revoked. This cycle continues until a Jini component cancels or fails to renew a lease. While a granted lease may not be revoked, lookup services may deny any lease request.

2.2.3 SLP. The Service Location Protocol (SLP) defines an architecture that enables clients, called user agents (UAs), and services, called service agents (SAs), to rendezvous through a third party, known as a directory agent (DA). The SLP architecture can be considered a hybrid because it allows UAs to discover SAs directly (two-party architecture) when a relevant DA (third party) cannot be found. The main discovery mechanism in SLP is an aggressive form of discovery, where UAs and SAs seek DAs by sending a specified number of probes on a multicast group at a designated interval. A UA is first required to probe for DAs. If no DAs are found during the probing period, then the UA may probe for SAs. SAs probe only for DAs. Each multicast probe contains a list of previous responders in order to allow potential responders to suppress duplicate replies. A SLP component periodically repeats the probing for DAs and SAs. Optionally, a SLP component may be provided a list of DAs to contact. Should a DA prove unavailable, a component can retry contacting the DA at a suitable interval. SLP also supports a form of lazy discovery because DAs and SAs periodically announce themselves; however, the announcement interval is configured by default to be rather large (about three hours), which makes SLP lazy announcement rather ineffective as a discovery mechanism.

A SLP SA registers a description of itself with each discovered DA. A SA requests registration for a TTL, which may be accepted by a DA. To extend registration, the registering SA must renew the registration prior to expiration of the TTL; otherwise, the DA revokes the registration. This cycle continues until the SA cancels or fails to refresh a registration. While an accepted registration may not be revoked prior to expiration of the TTL, a DA may deny any registration request. A UA may query any discovered DAs to find services of interest and to obtain attributes that describe services. If a UA cannot find any DAs, then the UA can issue a multicast search to find SAs, or to query SAs for available services. Unlike Jini, SLP provides no built-in means to allow a client (UA) to receive notification about service arrivals and departures or about changes in service descriptions. For this reason, SLP UAs must query DAs or SAs periodically to learn such information.

2.3 Example Service Discovery Architecture. In what follows, we take properties and concepts from existing SDP architectures as described in the previous section to derive a single coherent architectural framework necessary to understand subsequent sections of the paper. First, though, we introduce Figures 2-3 and 2-4 to describe a few concepts that must be encompassed by our formal model. Figure 2-3 extends the sample instance of a two-party service discovery architecture described above as Figure 2-1. The figure represents three network nodes (C1, S1, and S2), where each node executes one or more components. Node C1 contains two components: a client GUI component and a client service discovery entity (SDE). Node S1 and S2 each implement two components: a service provider and a ServiceProxy SDE. The service provider is the component that actually implements services offered to other components on the network, while the ServiceProxy SDE is the component the participates in the service discovery system on behalf of the service provider. (Note that a single ServiceProxy SDE might well act on behalf of multiple service providers.)

We denote a component as a SDE whenever it participates as a party in a service discovery system. Each SDE implements one or more roles associated with a service discovery function that defines a behavior, or series of action(s), intended to achieve an objective of a service discovery system, such as discovering directories or retrieving services. (We discuss specific service discovery roles and functions fully in section three and provide a simplified discussion here for illustrative purposes.) In our model, each function has two roles that complement each other. Roles identify initiators and recipients of messages; roles also identify the specific behaviors that cause messages to be sent and that occur in response to receiving messages. For example, Figure 2-3 illustrates a two-party service discovery system, where a client seeks services directly by issuing a query to a network multicast group. The client SDE implements one role (*Service Seeker*) to issue queries for services, while the ServiceProxy SDE implements a corresponding role (*Advertiser*) to respond to service queries issued by clients by returning a description of the service to the client.

SDEs participate in message exchanges either in (network-multicast) group form, such as when clients issue queries in Figure 2-3, or in direct form, which may be unidirectional, as shown in Figure 2-3, when service advertisers reply by sending service descriptions to clients. (Message exchanges may also be bi-directional as shown in Figure 2-4 when services or clients send a query to a directory that then replies with a directory description.) Group communication implies that any one of a set of allowed senders may transmit a message to be received by all of a set of subscribed receivers. Figure 2-3 illustrates a group that has one sender (C1: *Service Seeker*) and two receivers (S1: *Advertiser* and S2: *Advertiser*.) Figure 2-3 also includes two unidirectional direct message paths that allow the S1: *Advertiser* and the S2: *Advertiser* to each send a service description to the C1: *Service Seeker*.

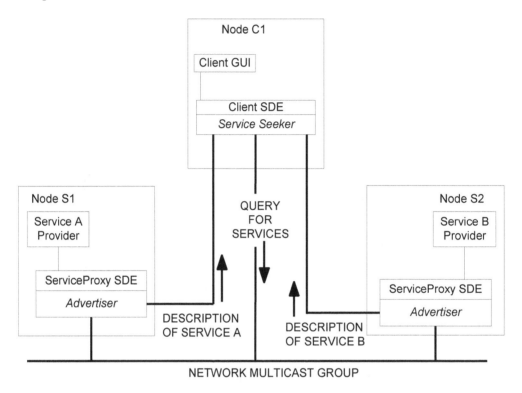

Figure 2-3. A Sample Two-Party Service Discovery Architecture with Distributed Components, Service Discovery Entities, and Service Discovery Roles

Figure 2-4, which extends the sample instance of a three-party architecture shown previously as Figure 2-2, illustrates how the complexity of a service discovery system can increase as parties, and associated functions and roles, are added to the design. For example, a three-party architecture requires that clients discover services through directories, which necessitates three distinct functions: repository discovery, followed by service registration and service retrieval. To perform these functions, the Directory SDE, located in node D1, is constructed with three roles: serving as a repository *Advertiser* in the repository-discovery function, acting as a *Service Registry* to allow services to be registered, and providing a service *Repository* from which services can be retrieved. The *Advertiser* sends directory announcements periodically on the network multicast group and listens for multicast queries for directories. The *Advertiser* must also listen for queries for directories sent directly from the complementary *Repository Seeker* roles, which are implemented in the Client SDE in node C1 and the ServiceProxy SDEs in nodes S1 and S2. Each *Repository Seeker* may issue multicast queries for directories and may send queries for directories to the *Advertiser* on any directory that announces itself on the multicast group. After obtaining a directory description, a ServiceProxy SDE initiates service registration by activating a *Service Registration Requester* to register a description of the service through the *Service Registry* associated with the discovered directory. A Client SDE initiates service retrieval after obtaining a directory description. The Client SDE activates a *Service Seeker* to query a *Repository* associated with the discovered directory. As will become clear in Section 3, SDEs may be composed of additional roles to implement further functions. As explained in Section 6, nodes may also implement multiple SDEs to act as various parties in a service discovery system.

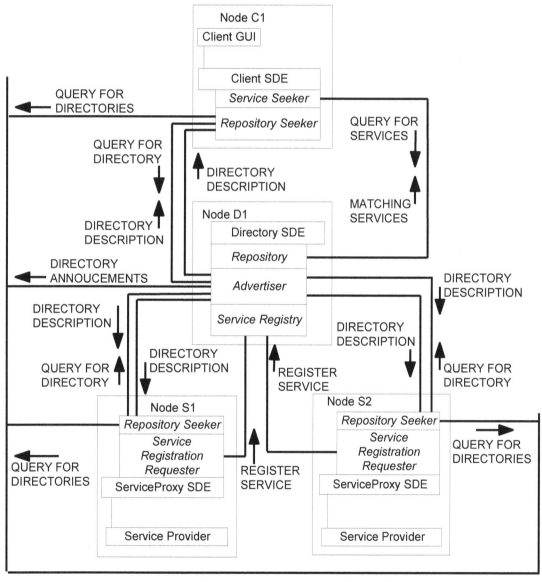

Figure 2-4. A Sample Three-Party Service Discovery Architecture with Distributed Components, Service Discovery Entities, and Service Discovery Roles

2.4 Formal Architectural Model. We represent the high-level concepts of our model as the UML diagram depicted in Figure 2-5. The model represents a service discovery system as an aggregation of SDEs; however, all SDEs need not be present. This highlights one challenging trait of the environment assumed by service discovery systems, that is, components participating in such systems can be present or absent at any time. This trait arises from the fact that SDEs are distributed components that execute on network nodes. Our model reflects this fact by representing each SDE as a subclass of `DistributedComponent` and by showing that each component executes on one network node, while a network node can support the execution of zero or more components. Our model assumes that a network node maintains three attributes: one describing node status and two describing the state of the node's network interface. The node itself may be either up or down, where down implies that none of the components supported by the node can execute; thus, are unreachable from components on other nodes. A node's transmitter and receiver may each individually be either up or down. When a node's transmitter is down, then all messages sent by components executing on the node will be lost. Similarly, when a node's receiver is down, all messages destined for components executing on the node will be lost. Since no specific component need be present on a network node, our model can also represent situations where some components on a node are unreachable while others are reachable.

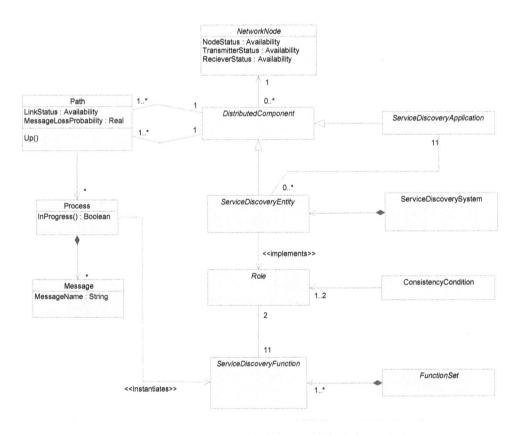

Figure 2-5. Top-Level Architectural Framework for
Generic Model of Service Discovery Systems

In our model, pairs of distributed components participate in processes that communicate over a path. A path, represented as the class `Path` in Figure 2-5, is a connection between exactly two instances of the class `DistributedComponent`. Figure 2-5 also shows that each `DistributedComponent` may participate in multiple paths. In addition, multiple processes, each comprising a set of messages, can coexist on a path. Each `Process` sends `Message`s on a path to execute a function, such as service discovery, service retrieval, or registration. The process type is defined by (1) the function it is executing and (2) the type of discoverable item for which the function is being performed, such as discovery of repositories or discovery of services. The Boolean `Path.up()` method returns TRUE if: (1) both sender and receiver exist, (2) the path between sender and receiver is operating, (3) the nodes containing sender and receiver are operating, and (4) all transmitters and receivers required for the process are operating. The Boolean `Process.inProgress()` takes arguments for a process and a path and returns TRUE if that process is active on the path.

The architectural examples shown in Figures 2-1 through 2-4 indicate that service discovery systems may rely on three different types of communication channels (multicast, unidirectional unicast, and bi-directional unicast) that we represent using the `Path` concept. Each instance of `Path` can represent two unidirectional unicast channels, and thus a bi-directional unicast channel. In our model, messages sent over a unicast channel flow directly from one specific sender to one specific receiver. Our model represents each multicast channel as a set of `Path` instances that may include any number of distributed components arrayed in any required configuration, such as a single sender and an arbitrary number of recipients. In our model, messages sent over a multicast channel flow from one specific sender to a set of one or more receivers.

Our model permits distributed components to be specialized as SDEs, where a SDE implements one or more service discovery roles, such as *Advertiser*, *Repository Seeker*, and *Service Seeker*. SDEs that implement roles exchange messages and thus participate in processes. Our model represents service discovery roles as UML (Unified Modeling Language) classes and relationships; messages correspond to class operation names. A set of operations and the behavior specified in the related methods compose a service discovery function, such as aggressive discovery, service registration, or change service. In our model, the messages and behavior associated with service discovery functions are modeled in UML sequence diagrams. In addition, related service discovery functions can be grouped into function sets, such as discovery, registration, or service retrieval. Our model represents function sets as UML packages. Section 3 describes the service discovery functions and roles contained within our model.

2.5 Specializing Service Discovery Entities through Service Discovery Roles. Our generic model can be used to represent specific service discovery systems. To do so, one represents the parties in a specific service discovery system as specializations of `ServiceDiscoveryEntity` (SDE) and then selects specific roles that each specialization will implement. For example, Figure 2-6 illustrates how this can be done to model the specific service discovery system shown in Figure 2-4.

Figure 2-6 shows three specialized SDEs: Directory SDE, ServiceProxy SDE, and Client SDE. Each specialized SDE implements the service discovery roles necessary to participate in selected service discovery functions; for example, the Client SDE implements two roles, *Repository Seeker* and *Service Seeker*, which allow the client to participate in the discovery of repositories and services. Implementing a particular service discovery role requires implementation of some mandatory classes and relationships (see Section 3), and may also allow implementation of some optional classes and relationships. Further, implemented classes may be subjected to normal object-oriented transformations, such as overriding and overloading methods. For example, a Client SDE that intends only to implement aggressive discovery would override (and nullify) methods associated with lazy discovery and directed discovery. Section 6 shows how to apply our generic model to represent selected service discovery systems.

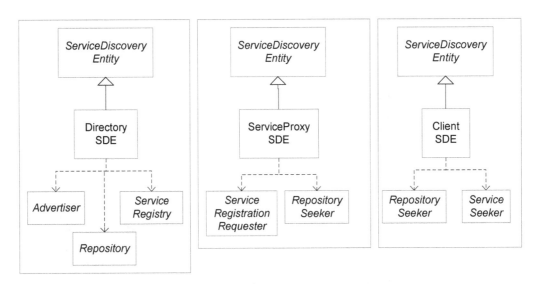

Figure 2-6. Model of Three-Party Service Discovery System Shown in Figure 2-4

2.6 Integrating with Service Discovery Applications. As represented in our generic model, SDEs provide support to service discovery applications (SDAs), which are also subclasses of `DistributedComponent`. For example, a Client SDE might discover repositories on behalf of a Client SDA, which could subsequently use a service-retrieval function implemented by the Client SDE to query discovered repositories. This pattern implies that SDEs cannot function alone, but instead must be linked to SDAs. Our model represents linkage among SDAs and SDEs using class methods (see Section 3.2.4). In some cases, a class method implemented by the SDE allows a SDA to initiate service discovery functions, while in other cases a class method must be implemented by a SDA to allow asynchronous notifications from the SDE. Typically, the linkage between SDE and SDA allows the SDA to detect dynamic changes within the topology of a service discovery system.

A SDA might wish to learn about the arrival and departure of repositories and services meeting specified criteria. A SDA might also wish to learn about changes in the criteria describing services and repositories previously discovered. In general, service discovery systems can adopt one (or both) of two mechanisms to detect such changes. One mechanism, *notification*, enables a SDE to emit an event to a SDA whenever: (1) a new description is discovered, (2) a known description is altered, or (3) a known description is deleted. To support notification, a SDA must inform a SDE of events of interest and provide a class method to receive notification when such events occur. A second mechanism, *polling*, requires a SDA to cache descriptions of interest, collected through SDE-provided methods, and then to periodically collect new copies of the descriptions. The SDA must compare the newly obtained descriptions with the previously cached copies in order to detect arrivals, departures, and changes. Selected SDAs may also use notification and polling provided by SDEs in order to detect changes in the state of variables maintained by service providers.

Change detection in service discovery systems is essential, not only because services can start and stop themselves gracefully, but also because nodes on which SDEs operate might crash and paths among SDEs might fail and then again become available. Due to the distributed and dynamic nature of service discovery systems, SDEs and SDAs might hold inconsistent information about available services and service state. For that reason, we define *consistency conditions* for roles associated with particular service discovery functions. Consistency conditions define basic requirements that service discovery systems should aim to satisfy in order to maintain consistent information about available services under dynamic conditions. These conditions also take into consideration that SDEs and SDAs may temporarily hold inconsistent information due to the effect of delays associated with failure detection and mitigation procedures, transmission latencies, and system deployment decisions. In Section 5, we use formal logic to specify the consistency bounds associated with our generic model. We argue that specifications for service discovery protocols would be improved if they included definitions of consistency bounds.

The continuous change and associated uncertainty that may exist in service discovery systems could present some performance problems. For example, issuing a query on a network multicast group that has an unknown population of potential respondents could initiate an implosion of responses that overrun the capacity of the query issuer. In a second example, an unknown population of components could attempt to register information with a directory and then renew those registrations at a frequency that overwhelms the capacity of the directory. In a third example, a large population of clients could discover a number of directory replicas against which to issue queries. Depending upon decisions taken by each client, some of the discovered directory replicas could be overwhelmed with queries, while others could remain under used. Among the service discovery systems we analyzed, these important, potential performance problems were not addressed. In Section 4, we discuss these problems and describe some algorithms that implementers of service discovery systems could adopt to improve performance. We also extend our UML model to represent the algorithms and supporting parameters.

3. An Object-Oriented Model of Service Discovery Systems

In this section, we describe and discuss key concepts, relationships, and behaviors composing our object-oriented, generic model of service discovery systems. We developed our model from analyses of selected, first-generation, service discovery protocols [1-7]. Our model expands on the architectural framework (including functions and roles) presented in Section 2 by providing: (1) class definitions to represent essential concepts and (2) sequence diagrams to depict key behaviors. Appendix A provides a full accounting of the function sets in our model. Each function set comprises specific, related functions. For each function, Appendix A identifies associated function roles and delineates model classes that must be implemented by each function role. Appendix A also indicates methods in specific model classes that are associated with particular functions. A full, machine-readable UML (Unified Modeling Language [26]) version of our model may be obtained by contacting us.

In what follows, we outline the fundamental elements of our UML model. A key feature of our model is separation between: (1) descriptions of different kinds of items that can be discovered and (2) various functions for discovering and monitoring those items. This separation means that, in principle, any of the discovery functions in our model can be used to find any of the discoverable items, though in practice specific discovery systems usually present more limited options. We begin by describing (in Section 3.1) the items within our model that can be found using discovery functions, and then we present (in Section 3.2) the three discovery functions our model provides to find items. To focus our description, we use an example of the discovery and monitoring of system-configuration information, as supported by selected first-generation service discovery systems. Third, we describe (in Section 3.3) how our model represents information registration, and permits extension of registrations. Fourth, we relate (in Section 3.4) procedures to discover and monitor service descriptions, the main discoverable item within our model, and the ultimate goal of service discovery protocols. Fifth, we discuss (in Section 3.5) how our model allows the discovery and monitoring of service variables. Finally, we identify (in Section 3.6) some design issues that appear inadequately addressed by the current, first-generation of service discovery systems.

3.1 Discoverable Items. In the following, we discuss the main discoverable items included in our model: service descriptions, repository descriptions, administrative scopes, and service types. We begin with service descriptions.

3.1.1 Service Descriptions. The main goal of a service discovery system is to locate a machine-interpretable characterization of services available on a network. We call such characterizations *service descriptions* (SDs), and represent them in our model by the class ServiceDescription. (See Figure 3-1 for a complete depiction of discoverable items as classes.) Each service description in our model encompasses a set of mandatory elements, and may also include a set of optional elements. Elements associated with a service description have two main purposes: (1) to enable discovery of services possessing particular characteristics and (2) to specify information necessary to invoke functionality provided by discovered services. Some elements in a service description also help to prevent the spread of stale information. In what follows, we assume the existence of SD:ServiceDescription, an instance of a service description.

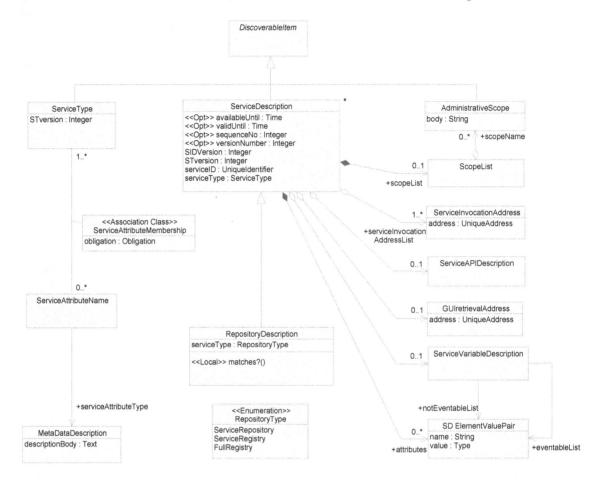

Figure 3-1. Class Diagram Depicting Discoverable Items

Every service has an identifier (SD.serviceID) that enables the service to be distinguished from all other services. In general, service identifiers should be unique over a global space and time. We assume that each service identifier refers to one or more service providers, each of which can create service instances if necessary. Our model allows service identifiers to be augmented with a version number (SD.SIDversion) to permit deployment of successive versions of the same service without need to assign a new service identifier. Service descriptions may include a list of administrative scopes (SD.scopeList) that restrict the visibility of services. (More on administrative scopes in a few paragraphs.) Every service also has an associated type (SD.serviceType) and optional version (SD.STversion), which uniquely identify attributes used to describe the service, i.e., that must or may be included in the service description. (Including a service-type version allows service-type names to be reused when revising the attributes associated with a service type.) For the list of included attributes (SD.attributes), the service description contains associated element-value pairs for each list item.

Our model allows each service description to include three pieces of information about the likely validity of the description. A sequence number (`SD.sequenceNo`) distinguishes among copies of the service description, which permits rejection of outdated copies and replacement of existing copies with newer copies. A validity timestamp (`SD.validUntil`) indicates the time after which a more recent copy of the service description should be sought, or alternatively a time after which the current copy may be discarded. An availability timestamp (`SD.availableUntil`) defines the intended closing time of the described service. The service should be available until the specified closing time. All the service discovery protocols that we studied confound these two concepts, description validity and service availability, into a single time-to-live field; however, we believe that the concepts should be distinguished because the validity of a service description is quite distinct from the intended availability of a service.

The remaining elements in our service description provide information necessary for a discovering entity to access the described service. Most important, each service description must include a list of one or more addresses (`SD.serviceInvocationAddressList`) through which client programs may invoke service methods. Many service discovery systems assume that service type implicates a description of service methods. Some service discovery systems permit service descriptions to include a list of method signatures. Our model provides an optional element (`SD.serviceAPIdescription`) in the service description to allow a service to include its method signatures. Selected services may provide a graphical user interface (GUI) in order to allow human users to access and interact with the service. Descriptions for such services might include an address (`SD.GUIretrievalAddress`) through which client programs can retrieve the GUI code; thus, our model includes this as an optional element.

Some services may expose a set of service variables that client programs can monitor. (In our model, service variables are distinct from service attributes, which change infrequently.) Each service variable in our model comes in one of two forms: (1) eventable and (2) non-eventable. Eventable service variables allow client programs to request notification of significant changes (events) related to variable value. Non-eventable service variables only permit client programs to query for variable values. Our model reflects the possibility that service variables can be described using one of two techniques. In one technique, a service provider can implement methods to retrieve lists of any eventable and non-eventable service variables offered by the provider, and to allow related event registration and notification and variable querying. In this case, the method descriptions are obtained in a manner similar to other methods offered by the service provider. In an alternate technique, a service provider may include lists of any eventable and non-eventable service variables directly in the service description. This alternate technique assumes that each service in the service discovery system provides standard methods to access and manipulate eventable and non-eventable variables. To allow for this alternate description, our model includes an optional element (`SD.serviceVariableDescription`) in our formulation of service description. A description of service variables includes a list of any eventable variables and a list of any non-eventable variables.

When fully specified with all options included, a service description in our model can become rather large. A similar situation arises in various service discovery systems. To better manage description size, some service discovery systems permit references (such as uniform resource locators, URLs) to be substituted for selected portions of a service description. Each substituted reference may be used by a discovering entity to retrieve the relevant missing portion of the service description. While not explicitly addressed in our model, we do not intend to exclude such substitutions. Specifically, we imagine that the following portions of our service description may be replaced by references to: (1) service attributes, (2) service method signatures, and (3) service variable descriptions. Designers of specific service discovery systems must consider the consequences of dividing an integral service description into pieces. Such a strategy has various pros and cons. To avoid discussing these tangential issues, we do not explicitly include substitutions in our formulation of service descriptions.

3.1.2 Repository Descriptions. While service descriptions encompass the main discoverable information in a service discovery system, a range of ancillary information might also be discoverable in order to support system configuration. For example, several service discovery systems allow clients and services to rendezvous through a third party, which we call a *repository*. In such systems, the first order of business for a client or service is to discover the existence of any repositories, which may contain collections of service descriptions. Discovering available repositories establishes the *physical extent* of a service discovery system. For this reason, our model includes a discoverable item *repository description*, represented as a subclass (`RespositoryDescription`) of `ServiceDescription`. Our model permits a repository description to contain any elements of a service description, but restricts the service type to be one of three values: `ServiceRepository`, `ServiceRegistry`, or `FullRegistry`. In our model, a *service repository* can only contain service descriptions related to services provided on the same (local) node that hosts the repository. Our model allows a repository that is a *service registry* to accept service descriptions for services hosted on other (remote) nodes. When extended from *service registry* to *full registry*, our model permits a repository to also accept client requests for notification of arrivals, departures, and changes of service descriptions. (We discuss service-description change monitoring in Section 3.4.)

3.1.3 Administrative Scopes. A number of other discoverable items relate to configuring the *logical extent* of a service discovery system. One such item, *administrative scope*, can be used to configure service discovery entities (SDEs) into distinct logical partitions, where each partition is defined by a scope name. When administrative scoping is employed, each SDE is assigned (or discovers) a list (`ScopeList`) of one or more scope names in which to participate. Our model interprets an empty list of scope names to designate any available scopes. Subsequent discovery messages (see Section 3.2) exchanged among SDEs include the list of scope names. Message recipients compare their own list of scope names with the list in each incoming discovery message. If the lists intersect, then the message can be processed; otherwise, the message must be discarded.

3.1.4 Service Types. Another discoverable item, *service type*, allows SDEs to discover the types (and versions) of any services available on a network (or within a logical partition of a network). A SDE can present the list of available service types to a user, or can use the list of available service types to formulate subsequent queries to find instances of services with specific attribute values (see Section 3.4). Recall that in our model (as in many service discovery systems) a service type is defined in terms of its mandatory and optional attributes, and attribute types. Formulating attribute-based queries relies on this relationship between service type and attributes. Most service discovery systems provide specifications that define the attributes associated with particular service types. In many cases, programmers of SDEs, and related service discovery applications (SDAs), encode the definition of service attributes, and their types, directly into application software. This approach limits a program to issue queries that include only mandatory attributes associated with a given service type, because services of the specified type need not implement any optional attributes. Some service discovery systems allow increased flexibility by supporting the discovery of service attributes (and service-attribute types) available for a given service type. This permits a SDE to discover what optional attributes, if any, are provided by available services that implement a specific service type. Once discovered, the optional attributes may be used within subsequent queries for services on the network. Our model supports the discovery of service attributes (`ServiceAttributeName`) and attribute types (`serviceAttributeType`) for a given service type. Our model also indicates whether an attribute is mandatory or optional (`ServiceAttributeMembership`), and allows each attribute type to refer to meta-data (`MetaDataDescription`). In this way, programs can discover the definition of attribute types. At a minimum, such definitions may be provided to human users to facilitate the construction of effective ad hoc queries. A further justification for including service types among the set of discoverable items is that the definitions of service types can change over time; thus, a dynamic means is needed to discover the most current version (and associated definition) for a service type.

3.2 Configuration Discovery and Monitoring. Upon initiation, SDEs need to understand the current configuration (i.e., the available, administrative scopes, service types, and repositories) of any service discovery system that might already be operating on the network. For systems that support administrative scopes, the first order of business for a SDE is to configure itself to use an appropriate set of scopes. Our model allows SDEs to use any of three approaches to configure scopes: (1) use a NULL scope list (denoting any scope), (2) use a locally configured scope list, and (3) use one of three primary discovery processes (explained below) to find administrative scopes available on the network. Primary discovery processes may be used in the absence of locally configured scopes, or to extend locally configured scopes. Once a SDE has configured its administrative scopes, the second order of business is to find any repositories that already exist on the network within those configured scopes. If no relevant repositories can be found, a SDE might then attempt to discover service types (and related attributes and types) in order to formulate queries that can be used to seek services directly (see Section 3.4).

Our model provides three, complementary, primary discovery processes: (1) lazy discovery, (2) aggressive discovery, and (3) directed discovery. Any of these discovery processes may by used to seek any discoverable item (i.e., administrative scope, service type, repository description, and service description). In lazy discovery, a SDE listens for announcements that may be multicast periodically to advertise descriptions of discoverable items. In aggressive discovery, a SDE sends multicast probes to solicit descriptions of discoverable items. In directed discovery, a SDE sends unicast probes to designated addresses to solicit descriptions of discoverable items. A SDE may use any or all of these discovery processes in combination, either simultaneously or serially, to seek administrative scopes, repositories, service types (and related attributes and types), as well as services. Figure 3-2 depicts some of the key model classes associated with seeking discoverable items.

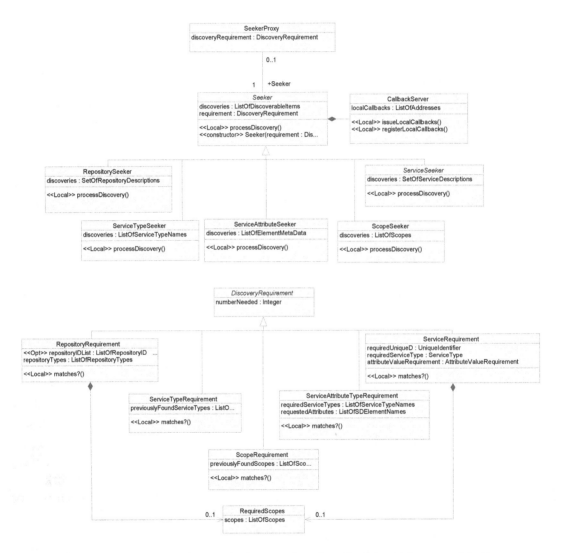

Figure 3-2. Classes and Associations Related to Seeking Discoverable Items

Our model includes an abstract class (*Seeker*) to initiate and control discovery processes, which are transient behaviors implemented by instances of another model class (SeekerProxy). Each instance of SeekerProxy can execute any of the discovery processes (either lazy, aggressive, or directed) with specified parameters, as supplied in related methods calls: listenForDiscovery(), seekDiscovery(), and contactAdvertiser(). *Seeker* provides *processDiscovery()*, an abstract method, which a SeekerProxy calls to convey detection of a discoverable item. *Seeker* includes a CallbackServer class that enables SDAs to register for notification of arrivals, departures, and changes to discoverable items. The CallbackServer class also enables the *Seeker* to issue notifications to registered SDAs. *Seeker* must be specialized to seek one type of discoverable item (RepositorySeeker, ServiceTypeSeeker, ServiceAttributeSeeker, ScopeSeeker, or ServiceSeeker). The specialization must include an appropriate override of *processDiscovery()*. Specializations of *Seeker* are constructed with a *DiscoveryRequirement*, which must be specialized to coincide with the particular subclass of *Seeker* that is instantiated. For example, a RepositorySeeker must be instantiated with a RepositoryRequirement, which can indicate a list of specific repository identifiers or repository types of interest and which can be optionally constrained to operate within specified scopes. For any *DiscoveryRequirement*, a *Seeker* may be constrained to find only a limited number of discoverable items matching the requirement. In what follows, we focus on repository discovery.

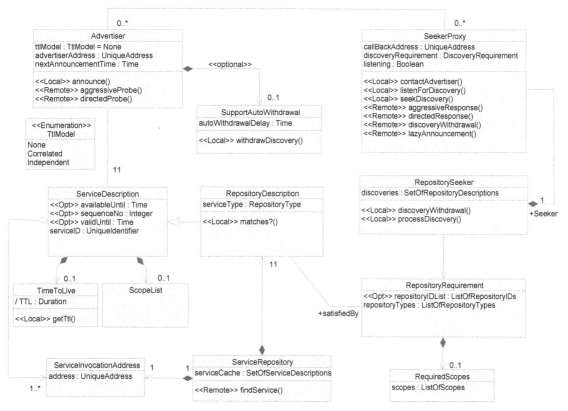

Figure 3-3. Classes and Associations Related to Seeking Repositories

Figure 3-3 illustrates the key model classes related to repository discovery. The right-hand side of the figure depicts relevant seeker classes, while the left-hand side of the figure introduces classes associated with a repository advertiser. In our model, an advertiser is responsible for announcing discoverable items (lazy discovery), and for responding to multicast (aggressive discovery) and unicast (directed discovery) probes from seekers. Advertisers in our model can be configured to reveal any of a range of discoverable items: a repository description, a list of administrative scopes associated with a repository, and a list of service identifiers or service types derived from service descriptions contained in a repository. In principle, a repository advertiser could also be configured to advertise administrative scopes derived from service descriptions contained in the repository; however, our model does not currently support this behavior because none of the discovery systems we analyzed properly handle the complex design issues related to overlapping administrative scopes (see Section 3.6.2). The model fragment shown in Figure 3-3 corresponds solely to advertisement of repository descriptions.

SDEs seek to discover repositories in order to query them for any cached service descriptions. As shown in Figure 3-3, a repository description describes a service repository that consists of a collection of service descriptions that can be accessed using the `ServiceRepository.findService()` method (see Section 3.4) at the invocation address contained in the repository description. The repository description (subclass of `ServiceDescription`) has an associated `Advertiser` class, an optional scope list, and an expiration time (`validUntil`) that denotes an absolute time after which the description may be outdated. Typically, clocks among distributed nodes are unsynchronized; thus, some service discovery systems communicate expiration times as a duration, or time-to-live (TTL), which can be computed by subtracting a node's local time from the expiration time. Upon receiving a TTL, the duration can be converted (by adding TTL to the local time) to an absolute expiration time aligned with the receiving node's clock. Our model represents TTL as an optional class (`TimeToLive`) that may be associated with service descriptions.

Our analysis of existing service discovery protocols uncovered various treatments of TTL. We included three treatments in our model. When conveyed in repository advertisements, a TTL indicates a duration after which the repository description might be outdated. In our model, `RepositoryDescription.validUntil` is used together with a specific algorithm to compute, using method `TimeToLive.getTTL()`, a TTL value to attach to repository descriptions in outgoing announcements. The method `TimeToLive.getTTL()` includes the following parameters: time of the next scheduled announcement (if any) and the TTL-computation algorithm (either *independent*, *correlated*, or *none*). The independent algorithm, which assigns TTL values unrelated to any planned periodic announcements of the repository description, computes the TTL value by subtracting the current time from `RepositoryDescription.validUntil`. Using this approach, repository seekers can continue to consider a repository description to be valid up until a locally computed (TTL added to current time) version of `validUntil`, even in the absence of periodic repository announcements. The correlated algorithm, which assigns TTL values to correspond with planned periodic repository announcements, computes the TTL value by subtracting the current time from the time the next repository announcement is due. Using this approach, repository seekers will invalidate cached copies of repository descriptions when anticipated periodic announcements are missed. If the algorithm is *none*, then a zero value is assigned for TTL. Given a TTL value of zero, a repository seeker must adopt local SDA policies to decide when to invalidate cached copies of repository descriptions.

3.2.1 Lazy Discovery. The UML sequence diagram given as Figure 3-4 illustrates how a repository seeker can detect a repository description using lazy discovery. In the advertiser, lazy announcement is initiated by a call to the `<<local>>`[1] method `Advertiser.announce()` with arguments that define: startup delay, announcement periodicity and distance, and, optionally, automatic withdrawal delay. An advertiser may send its lazy announcement messages over a specified distance (e.g., number of multicast hops). An advertiser may also be asked to delay for a time before beginning announcements. Once initiated, announcement occurs in cycles, where each cycle is separated by an announcement interval. Within each cycle, an advertiser may issue one or more multicast announcement messages, where each message is separated by an inter-message gap. Announcements may continue for a finite number of cycles or until availability ends (`RepositoryDescription.availableUntil`) for the repository description being announced. If the advertiser supports automatic withdrawal and the `Advertiser.announce()` method invocation includes an automatic withdrawal delay, then the advertiser will delay the specified time after the announcement cycle ends and issue an explicit withdrawal message to invalidate any cached copies of the advertised repository description. The example in Figure 3-4 shows invocation of the `Advertiser.announce()` method at a time T = 1000. After a 10s delay (at T=1010), two announcement cycles occur, one every 100s. Each announcement cycle consists of three announcement messages, each separated by 2s. Each lazy announcement message extends over 15 multicast hops. No automatic withdrawal delay is used.

The advertiser in Figure 3-4 uses a correlated TTL algorithm; thus, announcement messages include in the repository description a TTL correlated with the next anticipated announcement. Since only two announcement cycles are requested, repository seekers that cache copies of the announced repository description should invalidate those copies when an anticipated lazy announcement message fails to arrive at time 1210.

In Figure 3-4 each instance of a lazy announcement message invokes a `<<remote>>` method, `SeekerProxy.lazyAnnouncement()`, on every seeker proxy listening for lazy announcements about repositories. The method invocation conveys a repository description. In order to accept lazy announcements a seeker proxy must be enabled for listening. To start and stop listening for lazy announcements a seeker invokes the `<<local>>` method `SeekerProxy.listenForDiscovery()`. If listening is enabled, then for each incoming lazy announcement a seeker proxy invokes

---

[1] Our model uses the `<<local>>` stereotype to tag methods invoked from within the same SDE or SDE-SDA combination. We use the `<<remote>>` stereotype to tag methods exchanged among SDEs. In essence, `<<remote>>` methods model messages sent among objects via network protocols.

`Seeker.processDiscovery()`, where the disposition of the announcement is determined. If the (optional) sequence number in the repository description indicates stale information, then the announcement is discarded; otherwise, if the seeker has not previously discovered the repository and the quota for repositories is not satisfied and the repository description in the announcement matches the seeker's repository requirement, then the seeker adds the repository description to its cache. If the seeker has previously discovered the repository and the repository description still matches the seeker's repository requirement and the repository description includes a TTL, then the seeker updates its cached copy of `RepositoryDescription.validUntil` to reflect the new TTL value. If the seeker has previously discovered the repository and the current description no longer matches the seeker's repository requirement, then the seeker purges the cached repository description.

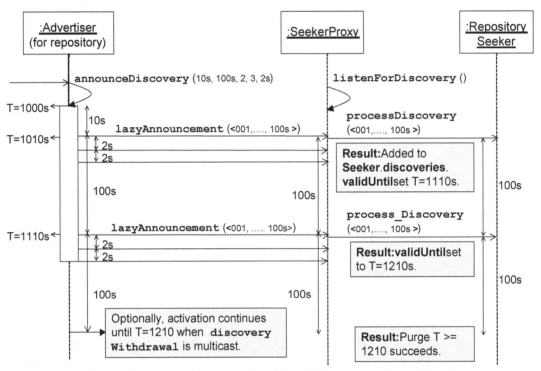

Figure 3-4. UML Sequence Diagram for a Lazy Discovery Example: Two announce cycles occur 100 s apart, with three announcements in each cycle. After initial caching, repository discovery is refreshed once, and then purged. The advertiser withdraws the repository after 1200 seconds of announcements.

3.2.2 Aggressive Discovery. The UML sequence diagram given as Figure 3-5 illustrates how a repository seeker can detect a repository description using aggressive discovery. During construction, a seeker proxy is provided with a discovery requirement that specifies characteristics of the discoverable item being sought. The seeker proxy will use this discovery requirement across all its possible discovery processes (i.e., lazy, aggressive, and directed). A seeker with multiple discovery requirements must construct multiple seeker proxies. In a seeker proxy, aggressive probing is initiated when a seeker calls the `<<local>>` method `SeekerProxy.seekDiscovery()` with arguments that define the probing periodicity, the probe distance (i.e., how far each probe should proceed before being removed from the network) and increase strategy, and the multicast response suppression and scheduling strategy (if any). Before commencing aggressive discovery, the seeker proxy checks the count of cached discoverable items. Discovery will be started only if the cache contains fewer entries than the seeker desires. Once initiated, probing occurs in cycles, where each cycle is separated by a cycle interval. Probing continues for a finite number of cycles, or until sufficient discoverable items are cached. Within each cycle, a seeker proxy may issue one or more multicast probe messages, where each message is separated by an inter-message gap. The probe distance indicates how far (in multicast hops) the first probe message should progress in the network. The increase strategy consists of (1) the number of additional hops to be added to the probe distance for each probe message and (2) the number of additional hops to be added to the probe distance for each probe cycle. Increasing probe distance over time permits a seeker to implement an expanding-ring multicast search, a strategy often adopted by discovery systems that prefer to find nearer discoverable items first.

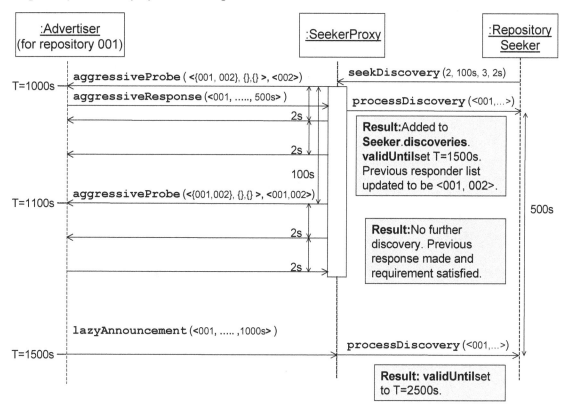

Figure 3-5. Using Aggressive Discovery to Seek a Repository with a Unique ID of 001. Two announce cycles occur 100 s apart, with three aggressive probes in each cycle. The : Advertiser for repository 001 responds, granting a TTL (=500 s), correlated to the lazy-announce cycle in which the next announcement occurs at T=1500 s. After initial caching, the discovery is refreshed by a subsequent announcement. The discovery may later be purged or withdrawn.

As illustrated in Figure 3-5 each instance of a multicast probe message invokes a `<<remote>>` method, `Advertiser.aggressiveProbe()`, on every advertiser listening for multicast probes. The method invocation conveys the following information associated with the current probe: the repository discovery requirement (which includes either a list of repository identifiers or a combination of repository types and scopes), and (an optional) list of already discovered items matching the discovery requirement. (The probe may also include some multicast response suppression or scheduling parameters, as discussed in Section 4.1.) The list of already discovered items allows a seeker proxy to convey the identity of items already found, which enables advertisers to suppress duplicate responses to successive multicast probes with identical discovery requirements. Upon receiving an aggressive probe, an advertiser will examine the list of already discovered items. If the advertiser has nothing to add, then no further action is required.

Next, an advertiser will compare its own characteristics against the discovery requirement; a match requires the advertiser to send a response to the return address (unless the availability of the discoverable item has expired). We represent the response message as a `<<remote>>` method, `SeekerProxy.aggressiveResponse()`, which includes the same parameters (recall 3.2.1) that the advertiser includes in lazy announcements of the discoverable item. Upon receiving the response, the seeker proxy applies the same processing as applied to incoming lazy announcements. If the response contains a newly discovered item, then the identity of the item will be included on the list of already discovered items (if used) in subsequent multicast probes sent by the seeker proxy. If the newly discovered item includes a TTL, then the seeker applies a purge policy to invalidate the cached item at the appropriate time. The seeker typically relies on lazy announcements (if used) to extend the TTL of cached items. The seeker is also free to initiate aggressive discovery in an effort to extend the TTL of cached items. If a cached item is purged, then the seeker is free to initiate aggressive discovery in an effort to find a replacement.

3.2.3 Directed Discovery. Directed discovery, which allows a seeker proxy to contact a pre-configured list of advertisers, uses unicast message transmission in place of multicast transmission. This approach might be necessary when operating on networks that do not support multicast routing or when attempting to discover advertisers at (administrative or physical) distances greater than can be reached through multicast. Directed discovery might also be advantageous when attempting to establish a wide-area topology of advertisers. As shown in Figure 3-6, directed discovery is initiated when a seeker calls the `<<local>>` method `SeekerProxy.contactAdvertiser()` with the list of advertiser addresses to contact, a retry interval, and (optionally) a maximum number of retries. The seeker proxy makes one attempt to contact each listed advertiser, removing any advertisers that were contacted successfully. If advertisers remain on the list, then, after the retry interval elapses, the seeker proxy makes another attempt to contact those advertisers. Retries continue until the maximum (if any) number of retries is reached, then the proxy seeker ceases attempting to contact advertisers.

For each advertiser that can be contacted, the seeker proxy invokes the `<<remote>>` method `Adverstiser.directedProbe()` with two parameters: (1) a return address to which responses can be sent and (2) a discovery requirement, against which the advertiser compares its own characteristics. If a match exists, then the advertiser invokes `<<remote>>` method `SeekerProxy.directedResponse()` with the same parameters that the advertiser includes in lazy announcements of the discoverable item. Upon receiving the response, the seeker proxy applies the same processing used for incoming lazy announcements. If the discoverable item is cached with a TTL, then the seeker exercises its local purge policy, which may include extending the TTL of the cached item as specified in any subsequent lazy announcements for the item. Of course, the seeker can be out of multicast range and fail to receive lazy announcements. For this reason, the seeker is free to initiate directed discovery as needed to extend TTLs and to recover purged items.

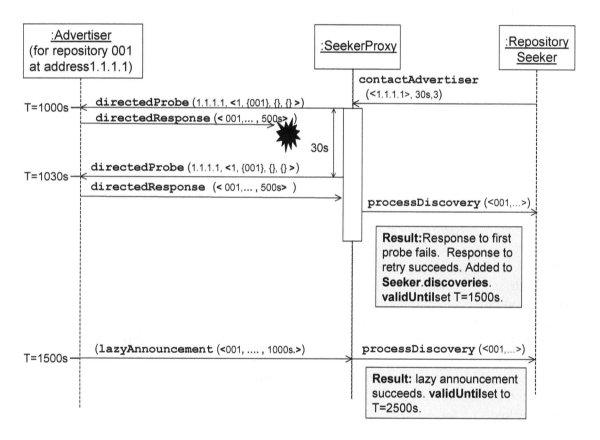

Figure 3-6. Using Directed Discovery to Seek a Repository at Address 1.1.1.1. Directed discovery is invoked to send up to three directed probes 30 s apart to the related `Advertiser`. Response to the first attempt fails due to network disruption. The `Advertiser` responds to the second attempt with a TTL (= 500 s) correlated to the lazy-announce cycle. After initial caching, the discovery is refreshed by a lazy announcement. The discovery may later be purged or withdrawn.

3.2.4 Monitoring Discoveries. Discovery processes include a monitoring aspect. As new discoverable items arrive on the network, the discovery processes result in additions to the caches maintained by SDEs. Such new discoveries will be conveyed by a seeker, using the method `CallbackServer.issueLocalCallbacks()`, as arrival events to all SDAs registered with the seeker to receive notification of new discoverable items. Similarly, previously cached discoverable items may be purged from SDE caches, either because a TTL expires, or because a withdrawal message (`SeekerProxy.discoveryWithdrawal()`) arrives, or because the SDE cannot obtain a later copy of the item. In any of these cases, the seeker issues departure events, as callbacks, to all SDAs registered to receive them. SDAs may also register with seekers to receive notification of changes to discoverable items. For example, a repository description might be cached with a specified set of administrative scopes. A subsequent lazy announcement of the same repository description could contain an altered scope list. In such a case, the seeker uses callbacks to issue change events to all SDAs registered to receive them. SDAs that do not register with a seeker to receive notice of arrivals or departures or changes can only learn about them by inspecting the SDE cache.

3.3 Registrations and Extension. After discovering a repository, a SDE might, depending upon repository type, be able to deposit information in the repository. For example, a service could deposit its service description, allowing other SDEs that discover the repository to also discover the service description. Clients could deposit notification requests to express the desire to be informed about changes to service descriptions contained within a repository. In addition, a SDE that discovers a service that provides eventable variables could deposit with the service a request for notification about changes in variable state.

Our model includes a registration process that enables SDEs to deposit information, which we call *registrations*, in a remote *registry*. The type of information that may be deposited depends upon the registry type: (1) service descriptions can be registered in service registries or full registries and (2) notification requests can be registered only in full registries. (A service repository does not accept remote registrations.) The registration process in our model is also used to register notification requests with services that provide eventable variables. Registration of service descriptions (and associated notification requests) supports a service discovery and monitoring process (see Section 3.4), while registration of requests for notification of changes to variable state supports a variable-monitoring process (see Section 3.5). In our model, registrations can occur for a limited duration, which may be extended periodically. This approach permits registries to detect failure of registering SDEs, and then to purge associated registrations; thus, limiting the period during which invalid information is disseminated to other SDEs in a service discovery system. In what follows we first describe our model of registrations and then discuss the registration process, followed by the extension process.

3.3.1 Registration Types. Figure 3-7 illustrates how our model represents registrations as classes. An abstract class (`Registration`) defines attributes common to all registrations, while concrete subclasses add additional information pertaining to specific types of registrations, including service descriptions (`ServiceRegistration`) and notification requests (`NotificationRegistration`) and requests for notification of changes in variable state (`ServiceVariableRegistration`). Each concrete class includes an association with a registration-request class that provides some of the attributes associated with the registration and that can be conveyed in registration-request messages (see Section 3.3.2). Registration-request messages also contain a request identifier (uniquely assigned by a registration requester to distinguish instances of registration requests) represented in our model as an attribute in an abstract class (*RegistrationRequest*). We take this approach as a convenient way to represent information that is included both in registrations and in messages (registration requests) that convey the registrations to registries.

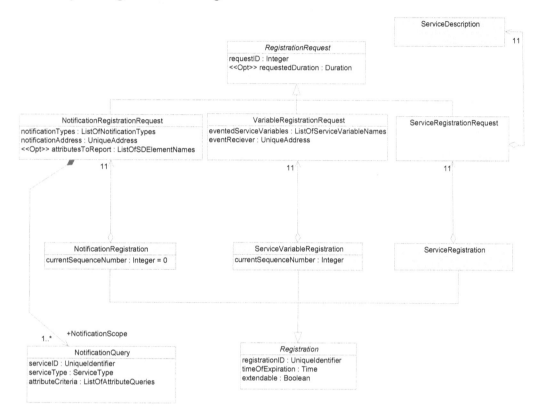

Figure 3-7. Class Diagram for Registration and Registration Requests

Every registration includes a unique identifier (assigned by the accepting registry) that can be exchanged among relevant classes to denote a specific registration instance. Each registration may also have a time of expiration used by registries in making purge decisions. Beyond these common attributes, a service registration includes only the service description being registered, while a notification registration includes the following information: (1) a list of notification types (i.e., service arrivals, departures, and changes) of interest to the registrant (an empty list denotes interest in any activity), (2) an address to which notifications should be sent, (3) an optional list of service attributes to include in notifications (if the list is empty, then an entire service description will be conveyed in each notification), (4) an optional set of notification queries, and (5) the sequence number assigned to the most recent notification sent about this registration. When a set of notification queries is present, each query restricts the terms of interest associated with a notification request. When the set is absent, a default query (which matches anything) is assumed. Some service discovery systems support a rather rich set of capabilities for expressing queries, while others restrict queries to service type or service identifier only. Our model allows each notification request to include a set of distinct queries, where each query in the set is logically connected together with disjunctions. For example, a registrant might be interested in a specific service type, in a specific service identifier, and in a service type that contains selected attributes (or selected attributes with some bounded range of values). In our model, these interests would be expressed as a set of three notification queries, where a match against any one (or more) of the queries would lead to a related notification. Notification requests associated with eventable variables are somewhat less complicated, including the common attributes (registration identifier and time of expiration), an address to which notifications should be sent, the sequence number of the most recent notification associated with the registration, and a list containing the specific eventable variables of interest to the registrant (an empty list denotes interest in all eventable variables offered by a service).

3.3.2 Registration Process. Our model includes an abstract class (`Registry`) that defines methods that must be implemented by classes wishing to accept registrations. Our model also provides the abstract class `RegistrationRequester`, which must be specialized by classes wishing to request specific types of registrations. Figure 3-8 depicts these abstractions, along with specific concrete classes and interfaces defined in our model to support registration of service descriptions and notification requests (for both services and variables). Each concrete class overrides the abstract methods as necessary to process a specific type of registration. Here, we define the abstract behavior (shown in Figure 3-9) associated with the registration process included in our model.

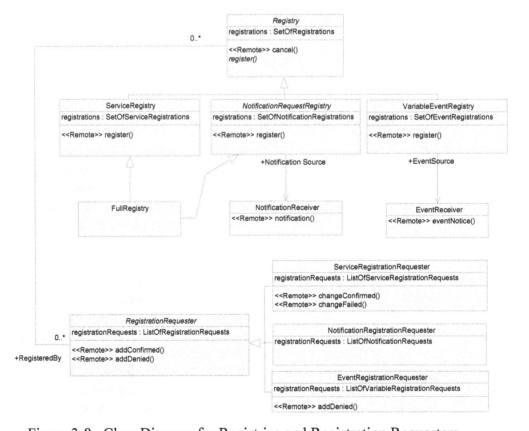

Figure 3-8. Class Diagram for Registries and Registration Requesters

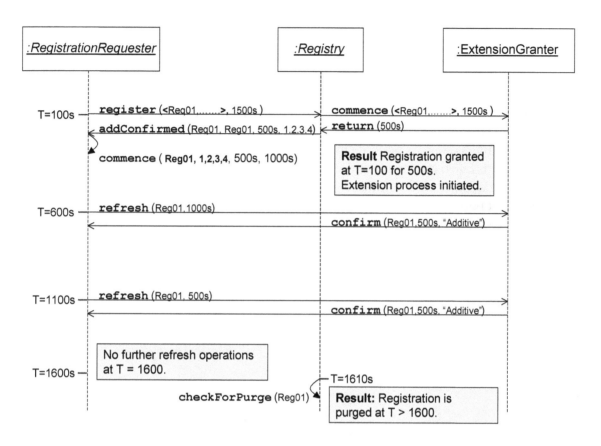

Figure 3-9. Abstract Behavior for Registration and Extension. An initial registration requesting 1500 s is granted for a period of 500 s. Since the granted time is less tha   n the requested time, the   `RegistrationRequester`, which implements the `ExtensionRequester` interface, requests and obtains two additional extensions for the remaining time using the additive strategy (see below). After expiration of the second extension, the `Registry` purges the registration.

To initiate the registration process, a registration requester invokes the   `<<remote>>` method `Registry.register()` with input parameters: `RegistrationRequest` and (optional) requested duration. (Some service discovery systems implement default registration durations and, so, do not include a requested duration in registration requests.) Subject to capacity constraints, the   `register()` method assigns a registration identifier and adds the registration to the registry. As part of this process, an extension granter is consulted (see Section 3.3.3) to assign an expiration time to the new registration. A registry will periodically check its set of registrations, purging those that have expired. If a registration is successfully added, then the registry invokes a `<<remote>>` method `RegistrationRequester.addConfirmed()`, conveying the associated request identifier, the newly assigned registration identifier, a granted time-to-live (TTL) for the registration, and the address of an extension granter through which to request extensions to the granted TTL. If a registry chooses to reject a registration request, then the requester is notified through a   `<<remote>>` method

RegistrationRequester.addDenied(), which conveys the associated request identifier and a reason for denying registration. By invoking a `<<remote>>` method *Registry.cancel()* with the registration identifier, a registration requester can cancel a confirmed registration prior to expiration of a granted TTL.

3.3.3 Extension Process. In many situations, a registrant may wish a registration to be valid for an extended period of time. On the other hand, a registry might desire to detect registrant failure as soon as possible in order to reclaim space from registrations associated with failed registrants and to limit the time during which the registry supplies invalid information to other entities in a service discovery system. Thus, registries are likely to grant registrations with shorter TTL than requested. Our model includes classes (see Figure 3-10) implementing an extension process that can be used to resolve differences between requested and granted TTL.

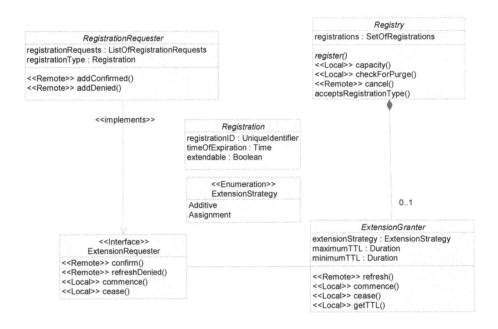

Figure 3-10. Class Diagram for Registration Extension

To obtain an initial granted TTL for a registration, a registry invokes a `<<local>>` method *ExtensionGranter.commence()* with an input registration identifier and a requested TTL (if any). A granted TTL, computed by `<<local>>` method *ExtensionGranter.getTTL()*, is used to update the expiration time of the associated registration, and is returned to the registry. The registry passes the granted TTL (and the address of the extension granter) to the registration requester as part of the message confirming registration.

To extend a granted TTL (see UML sequence diagram Figure 3-9), a registration requester must implement an interface, `ExtensionRequester`, which provides methods to interact with a remote class, *ExtensionGranter*, associated with a registry. Upon receiving an initial granted TTL, a registration requester can compute the difference from the requested TTL. If the computed difference exceeds zero, then the registration requester can invoke `ExtensionRequester.commence()`, a `<<local>>` method with input parameters: registration identifier, address of an extension granter, the granted TTL, and the additional requested TTL. Prior to expiration of the granted TTL, the extension requester invokes a `<<remote>>` method `ExtensionGranter.refresh()` with parameters: registration identifier and requested extension duration. The registration granter calculates a TTL extension, if any, and updates the expiration time of the associated registration, returning the extended TTL via `<<remote>>` method `ExtensionRequester.confirm()`, which has parameters registration identifier, granted TTL duration, and extension strategy (either additive or assignment). When updating the expiration time of a registration, an extension granter may use one of two strategies. An additive strategy adds the extended TTL to the current expiration time associated with the registration. An assignment strategy adds the extended TTL to the current time and then overwrites the previous expiration time associated with the registration. The strategy used by the extension granter must be conveyed to the extension requester in order to properly use the granted TTL duration. If an extension refresh is not requested (or not granted), then a registry will eventually purge the expired registration.

Service discovery systems can employ various algorithms to determine how much TTL extension to grant for each request. Our model accommodates such variations by encapsulating the specific algorithms in an abstract `<<local>>` method, `ExtensionGranter.getTTL()`, which, given a requested TTL, returns a granted TTL extension. The class `ExtensionGranter` includes some attributes that bound the (minimum and maximum) TTL to grant. In a subsequent section (see Section 4.2) on performance considerations, we describe alternate algorithms for computing the TTL.

Upon receiving an extended TTL, the extension requester determines if additional extension is required, then, if necessary, schedules another call to `ExtensionGranter.refresh()` just prior to the expiration time computed from the granted TTL and extension strategy. In general, an extension granter need not honor requests to extend a registration TTL; the `<<remote>>` method `ExtensionRequester.refreshDenied()` is invoked to convey the negative decision for an associated registration identifier and giving an optional reason for the denial. For example, a request for extension might arrive too late at the extension granter, which will find no corresponding registration because the registry may already have purged the record. In this case, the extension granter calls a `<<remote>>` method `ExtensionRequester.refreshDenied()` with the registration identifier and with `unknown_registration` as the reason for denying the requested extension.

Registration extension should be halted whenever an associated registration is invalidated, which occurs when a registry receives a request to cancel, or decides to purge, a registration. Upon deciding to cancel a registration, a registration requester should invoke `ExtensionRequester.cease()` with the associated registration identifier. A registry invokes *ExtensionGranter.cease()* with a specific registration identifier to halt granting extensions for the registration.

3.4 Service-Description Discovery and Monitoring. Given that the main task of clients in service discovery systems is to find and monitor service descriptions, the specific discovery and monitoring techniques available depend upon whether or not repositories can be discovered. If repositories are found, then clients and services can interact through repositories; otherwise, clients and services must interact directly. In what follows, we discuss how our model supports the discovery and monitoring of service descriptions under these two different conditions. First, we describe how our model supports service-description discovery and monitoring with repositories. Second, we consider how our model represents service-description discovery and monitoring without repositories.

3.4.1 Service-Description Discovery with Repositories. Previous sections described how services and clients could discover repositories (see Section 3.2) and how services could deposit service descriptions (see Section 3.3.2) with discovered repositories. In this section, we focus on our model for clients to retrieve service descriptions from repositories. We call this secondary discovery, because first a repository is found (using primary discovery processes) and then the repository is queried for service descriptions. As shown in Figure 3-11, our model includes an abstract class, *ServiceSeeker*, which provides several attributes: service requirement, an indication of whether service requirements are compared and filtered (i.e., matched) remotely (on the repository) or locally (on the service seeker), and a cache for service descriptions matching the service requirement. A ServiceRequirement (subclass of *DiscoveryRequirement*) specifies the traits in service descriptions of interest to a service seeker. Service requirements may specify a service identifier or a service type and optional set of service attributes (and possibly ranges of values for each attribute). Service descriptions may be compared against the traits of a service seeker's service requirement; matching service descriptions are retained in the service seeker's local cache. In our model, a service seeker has only one service requirement; thus, to look for service descriptions matching multiple service requirements a client must start additional service seekers. *ServiceSeeker* includes an abstract <<local>> method, processDiscovery(), which must be implemented to cache newly discovered service descriptions. If local matching is used, then processDiscovery() must first compare an input service description for a match against the local service requirement.

To retrieve service descriptions from repositories, *ServiceSeeker* is specialized to a class, UnicastServiceSeeker, which provides a <<local>> method, issueFindService(), to initiate the sending of unicast queries to known repositories that have been discovered previously. In our model, <<remote>> method ServiceRepository.findService() represents a unicast query arriving at a repository with parameters: a service requirement, an address to receive any matching service descriptions, an optional set of requested attributes (used to restrict the contents of any service descriptions returned to the service seeker), and an optional limit on the number of matching service descriptions to be returned. When a service seeker wishes to filter locally for matching service descriptions, then the findService() includes a

NULL service requirement (matching any service description). To return matching service descriptions to the service seeker, a repository invokes a `<<remote>>` method `serviceFound()` provided by the `UnicastServiceSeeker`. The method is invoked with the following parameters: a set of service descriptions (each optionally including a TTL) that match any restrictions included in the find-service query, the repository identifier returning the service descriptions, and an optional number of additional matching service descriptions not returned by the repository. Using this last parameter, a service seeker may decide to issue another query to gather additional matching service descriptions. Service descriptions that have a TTL (calculated as discussed previously in Section 3.2) advise a service seeker to establish a local time after which to seek an updated copy of cached service descriptions that may be outdated. Absent a TTL, the service seeker must use a local policy to decide when to update (or purge) cached copies of service descriptions.

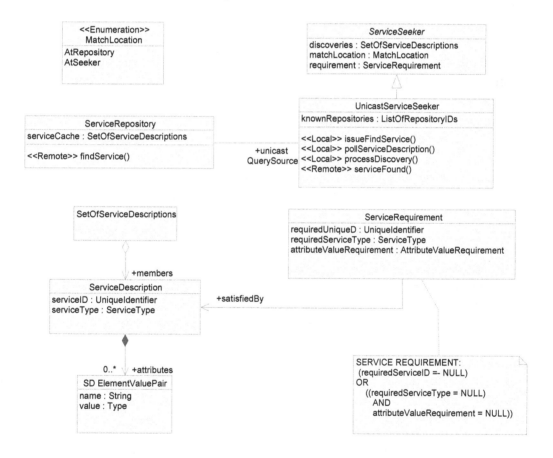

Figure 3-11. Class Diagram for Service Retrieval with Repositories

Whether or not any matching service descriptions are found on a repository, a client might be allowed to register (see Sections 3.3.1 and 3.3.2) a request with the repository to be notified if any service descriptions matching the requirement arrive at the repository. In this case, the service requirement is included as part of the notification request. Note that notification requests permit service requirements to be aggregated together. Also note that clients in service discovery systems should issue a find-service request to a repository following registration of a request for notification of service arrivals. This permits detection of service arrivals that occur over the interval during which the registration is being processed.

3.4.2 Service-Description Monitoring with Repositories. Repositories may be monitored to detect changes in, or departures of, previously discovered service descriptions. Our model supports two change-detection techniques: *notification* and *polling*. Below, we discuss each of these in turn.

3.4.2.1 Notification. In previous sections (see Sections 3.3.2 and 3.3.3), we described how service descriptions might be purged from repositories when a TTL expires or when cancelled by a service. Here, we discuss how repositories can notify clients of such departures, as well as changes to the content of registered service descriptions. First, though, we describe how our model allows a service to change the content of a service description already registered with a repository.

Figure 3-8 illustrates the classes and relationships in our model related to service registration: abstract classes `Registry` and `RegistrationRequester` are specialized as `ServiceRegistry` and `ServiceRegistrationRequester`, respectively. Service registry includes `changeServiceDescription()`, a `<<remote>>` method invoked to update a service description previously deposited on a registry. Our model allows attributes to be added and deleted from registered service descriptions, and also allows the values of attributes to be changed. Any of these alterations amount to a *change* to a registered service description. Requests to change a service description include the following parameters: the address of an object (implementing the service-registration requester methods) that will accept results, a registration identifier (to indicate the relevant service description), a change identifier (which is a sequence number to ensure that stale changes are not allowed to overwrite more recent information), an action (add, delete, or change), and a list of attributes to alter (which include attribute values when the action is add or change). Our model restricts each invocation of the change-service method to convey only a single type of action; thus, more complicated alterations to a service description must be represented as a sequence of operations. Upon successfully completing a requested change-service operation, a service registry invokes `<<remote>>` method `changeConfirmed()` on the indicated address, returning the registration and change identifiers and any delay until the change becomes effective. If a service registry cannot successfully complete the requested change to a service description, then it invokes `<<remote>>` method `changeFailed()` on the indicated address, returning the registration and change identifiers and a reason for the failure.

Successful completion of a change-service request leads a service registry to attempt to notify any (and all) objects registered to receive such information. Recall (Section 3.3.2) that objects may register to receive notification of arrivals, changes, and departures involving service descriptions. Figure 3-12 provides a UML sequence diagram that portrays events related to an initial service registration, notification of the service arrival, a subsequent change-service request, and related notification of the change to the service description. Similar event sequences (not shown) occur when cancellation of a service registration leads to notification of the service departure.

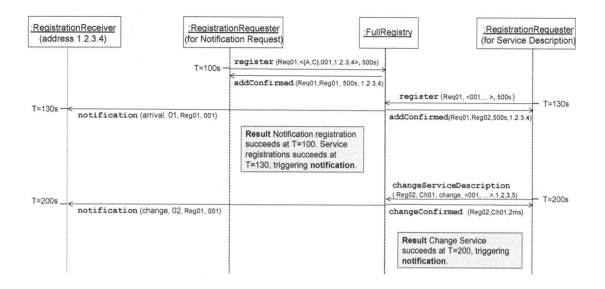

Figure 3-12. Registration and Notification: A `RegistrationRequester` registers with a `FullRegistry` for notification of *arrival* and *change* of `ServiceDescription` 001, denoted by {A, C}. Another `RegistrationRequester` subsequently registers this service description, and the registry issues an *arrival* `notification()` to the `NotificationReceiver` designated at address 1.2.3.4. The `RegistrationRequester` for the service description subsequently issues a `changeServiceDescription()`, which triggers a *change* `notification` to the `NotificationReceiver`. Optionally, if *departure* notification had been requested, purge of `ServiceDescription` 001 would also trigger a notification.

3.4.2.2 Polling. Some service discovery systems do not include mechanisms to notify interested parties about arrivals, departures, and changes to service descriptions on repositories. In such systems, clients may only detect arrivals, departures, and changes by periodically polling for service descriptions. Typically, a client will periodically query (using a unicast find-service request) a repository to discover a service description of interest. After retrieving and caching a service description, a client can then periodically query a repository for the latest copy of the service description, comparing the new copy with the previously cached version to detect any attribute changes. If a client can no longer obtain a copy of a previously cached service description, then the client could infer that the repository no longer holds the description. While these polling procedures are application-programming decisions taken by a client SDE, our model of the class `UnicastServiceSeeker` provides `pollServiceDescription()`, a `<<local>>` method to initiate a polling process on behalf of a client. The method includes input parameters: repository identifier (to poll), service identifier (of the service description of interest), an optional list of requested attributes (if not provided, then the whole service description is retrieved), a polling interval, and the number of polls to attempt. The method must also annotate the cached service description of the indicated service identifier to record the fact that polling operations are underway. In our model, the method `ServiceSeeker.processDiscovery()` must also be overridden to consult the polling indicator associated with the incoming service identifier and then, if necessary, to compare an incoming service description with a previously cached copy to detect any attribute changes. Since multiple repositories may have been discovered, a seeker has the option of querying only one repository with each poll. In Section 4.3 we describe some approaches that a seeker may use to select a target for each poll.

3.4.3 Service-Description Discovery without Repositories. Some service discovery systems do not permit repositories. Even when permitted, repositories might be unavailable. For these reasons, some service discovery systems provide mechanisms through which clients can attempt to discover services directly through multicast queries. Our model permits `ServiceSeeker` to be specialized as `MulticastServiceSeeker`, which uses aggressive discovery procedures to issue multicast queries containing a service requirement and which also uses lazy discovery procedures to listen for any announcements of service descriptions. We found no service discovery protocols that issue multicast announcements containing a full service description; however, we did find a few service discovery protocols that issue multicast announcements of service identifiers and service types, where each announcement contains an address where a full service description may be obtained. The procedures described previously for aggressive and lazy discovery (recall Sections 3.2.1 and 3.2.2) are the same procedures used in our model to represent multicast queries and announcements associated with discovery of service descriptions.

3.4.4 Service-Description Monitoring without Repositories. Absent a repository, departure of service descriptions can be detected in the same way as departure of other discoverable items. Service descriptions might have an associated TTL, which will lead a client to purge the service description if a new announcement does not arrive in time to extend the TTL (see Section 3.2.1). Alternately, a `MulticastServiceSeeker` might receive an indication, `discoveryWithdrawal()`, when a service is withdrawn. Of course, a client might also use a local policy (such as repeated failure to connect) to purge a cached service description. Absent repositories, detecting change in the attributes of previously discovered service descriptions depends upon clients implementing a polling scheme along the lines described in Section 3.4.2.2, but polling the provider of the service description instead of a third-party repository holding registered service descriptions. Of course, a service provider is free to implement methods or variables that might provide indication of changes in service-description attributes.

3.5 Variable Discovery and Monitoring. Some service discovery systems include specific procedures for service providers to make variables, both eventable and non-eventable, available to clients. For this reason, we decided to include such procedures as an option within our model. Figure 3-13 contains key classes associated with variable discovery and monitoring in our model. A service provider must implement an optional class, `VariableProvider`, to make variables accessible to clients. The class provides two

<<remote>> methods, getEventableVariables() and getMonitorableVariables(), which enable a client to retrieve a list of the eventable and non-eventable variables, respectively. Each method includes only one parameter, an object address to which variable lists should be returned. To receive variable lists, a client must implement the class VariableAccessor, which includes <<remote>> methods to receive asynchronous results from the list queries. These methods are called by a variable provider to return a list of non-eventable variables (monitorableVariablesFound()) or a list of eventable variables (eventableVariablesFound()).

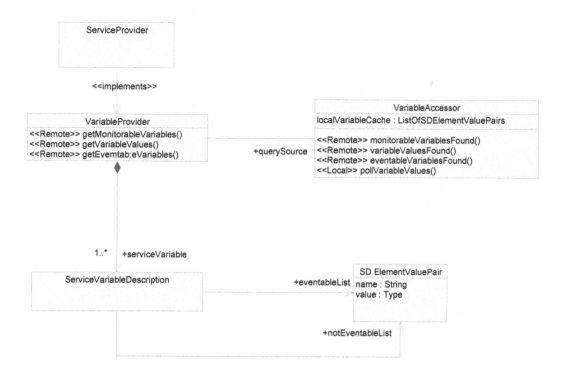

Figure 3-13. Class Diagram for Variable Monitoring

The variable-list retrieval methods are optional for a variable provider because some service discovery systems include a list of the eventable and non-eventable variables (see Section 3.1) in the service description. For service discovery systems that do not include service variables in the service description, variable-list retrieval methods permit a client to obtain a list of available service variables in each category (eventable and non-eventable). Our model, then, includes two alternate approaches to find service variables: by discovering a service description or by getting lists of service variables directly from a service provider. Once found, service variables may be monitored using queries (for non-eventable variables) or notifications (for eventable variables). We first discuss queries and then notifications.

A mandatory <<remote>> method, getVariableValues(), implemented by a variable provider, enables a client to submit a list of variables for which values are requested to be returned to a designated address. The input variable list represents a one-time query for the current values of the variables on the list. To receive the variable values, a client must implement `<<remote>>` method, `variableValuesFound()`, which is called by a variable provider to convey a list of variable values. A client may use periodic queries (as discussed in Section 3.4.4.2) to monitor variable values. The `VariableAccessor` class includes a `<<local>>` method, `pollVariables()`, to initiate a period of variable polling. When polling, a client must provide local logic to cache variable values and to compare newly received values to previously cached values to detect when the value of a variable changes.

When a service provider offers eventable variables, a client has the option to register for notification of changes in variable state. In our model, these procedures build on the registration, extension, and notification processes discussed previously. Figure 3-8 identities the classes and relationships included in our model to represent eventable-variable registration and notification. As shown, the abstract `Registry` class is specialized by a concrete class, `VariableEventRegistry`, which overrides the abstract registration methods to handle an appropriate kind of registration request, `VariableRegistrationRequest`, which specializes the abstract class `RegistrationRequest`. Variable-registration requests include a list of eventable variables that a client is interested in monitoring and the address of an `EventReceiver` to notify when a change occurs in the state of one or more of the designated variables. Our model makes no statement about what constitutes a change in variable state. To convey an event, a variable-event registry invokes a `<<remote>>` method `EventReceiver.eventNotice()` with the following parameters: registration identifier, service identifier, sequence number, and a list of eventable variables (and their current values) that have changed. When an event occurs, the variable-event registry attempts to inform any (and all) event receivers registered for event notices.

To register for notice of variable events, in our model a client must implement a concrete class, `EventRegistrationRequester`, which inherits from abstract class `RegistrationRequester` and overrides registration-result methods as necessary. One required override adds a reason, `requested_variable_not_monitorable`, to the list of reasons that can be used to deny a registration. In our model, variable-event registration uses the optional extension process (see Section 3.3) to continue registrations beyond an initially granted duration.

3.6 Limitations and Open Issues. The set of first-generation service discovery systems we analyzed exhibited some limitations that lead directly to six open issues in our model. First, our model reflects the fact that first-generation service discovery systems are designed for use at limited scale. Second, our model reflects the fact that first-generation service discovery systems provide an incomplete design for logical partitioning. Third, our model reflects the fact that first-generation service discovery systems do not support notification about changes in repository descriptions. Fourth, our model reflects the fact that first-generation service discovery systems do not clearly distinguish between the role of a service provider and the role of a proxy that participates in service discovery processes on behalf of the service provider. Fifth, our model reflects the fact that first-generation service discovery systems do not define eventable variables with sufficient detail. Sixth, our model reflects the fact the first-generation service discovery systems do not consider deployment on resource-constrained devices. We address each of these issues in turn.

3.6.1 Limited Scalability. In the first-generation of service discovery systems that we analyzed, clients and services could discover a set of repositories through which to rendezvous. Unfortunately, none of the service discovery systems we examined define any relationship (save replication and partition) among the multiple repositories that might exist. This means that in a global system, a service and client may rendezvous only by discovering the same repository (or one of its replicas). This design places severe restrictions on the ability of a discovery system to reach a global scale. Either clients or services must be capable of discovering every repository in a global network, or repositories must be capable of discovering each other and organizing into topologies. The current generation of service discovery protocols provides only two approaches to accomplish this feat: (1) use lazy or aggressive multicast discovery to find repositories and (2) use directed discovery to find a set of known repositories. The multicast approach can lead to dissemination of an excessive number of multicast messages in a large network, because multicast lazy announcements must extend throughout the entire network, reaching every available client and service. If aggressive discovery adopts an expanding ring multicast search and stops at the first discovered repository, then the population of services and clients will form into numerous geographically partitioned collections, which would not enable global service discovery. To avoid such partitions, aggressive discovery multicast messages must also extend throughout the entire global network. On the other hand, each client or service could be given a list of all (or most) of the repositories available in the network and then contact them directly and interact with each of them. Of course, this approach exhibits some significant practical problems. First, how is the list of repositories accumulated and provided to each client or service in the global network? Second, how is the list updated as new repositories arise? Third, how can every client or service interact with every repository in the global network without placing undue processing load on the client or service and repository? Our current model reflects these scalability limitations inherent in first-generation service discovery systems. On-going research [27-32] in future service discovery systems investigates techniques that permit repositories to self-organize into topologies that support wide-area search, so that a client or service need only discover one repository to obtain access to the global set of services offered throughout the network. Such self-organizing wide-area search systems also aim to support reorganization with changes in the population of services and repositories.

3.6.2 Incomplete Design of Logical Partitioning Schemes. Of the service discovery systems that we analyzed only two support logical partitioning schemes, which enable components to be classified into distinct collections based upon administrative scopes. In effect, each component may be assigned membership in one or more administrative scopes, and then components may only discover each other when their administrative-scope membership intersects. To this extent, we include administrative scoping in our model of first-generation service discovery systems. One of the protocols we analyzed supports this limited form of administrative scoping by requiring that each component establish its scope list at startup and then not change scope membership during the component's lifetime.

Another of the protocols we analyzed provides the ability for a component to change scope membership dynamically during execution, which could allow clients and services that acquire additional administrative scopes to initiate aggressive or directed discovery to find related repositories. Similarly, repositories that acquire additional scopes could announce this change to potential repository seekers. The specification we analyzed requires clients and services to deregister notification requests and service descriptions, respectively, from repositories that fall out of scope. In cases where scope membership is reduced, the service discovery system that supports Unfortunately, the specification does not require a repository to associate registered service descriptions and notification requests with specific administrative scopes; thus, when the scope membership of a repository is reduced no direct action can be taken to remove service descriptions and notification requests that fall out of scope, or to notify registrants about the scope reduction. Of course, a later announcement from the repository might lead repository seekers to discard the associated repository description, should the repository fall out of scope. In effect, approach limits administrative scoping to discovery processes only, whereas a more complete design would associate administrative scoping with registration as well.

We decided to exclude dynamic scope changes from our model, because only one of the service discovery systems we analyzed allowed such behavior and that system did not fully realize a complete design that associates registrations with administrative scopes. We believe that a complete design for administrative scoping could empower scope changes to dynamically reorganize the logical topology of executing service discovery systems. To accomplish this would require associating administrative scopes not only with discovery processes but also with registration processes. A complete design would also require defining appropriate behaviors to be taken by repositories, clients, and services in reaction to changes in local administrative scope. Since none of the service discovery systems we analyzed provided a complete design for dynamic changes of administrative scope, we omitted such functionality from our model.

3.6.3 Unsupported Notification of Changes to Repository Descriptions. Our model represents repository descriptions as a subclass of service description. Given such representation, one would expect that repository seekers could register for notification about updates to a repository description. Such updates might include changes in: scope, repository capabilities (e.g., `ServiceRegistry` or `FullRegistry`), or invocation address (as might occur in mobile networks). None of the service discovery systems that we analyzed supports dynamic change and notification for repository descriptions. For this reason, we omitted such beneficial functionality from our model.

3.6.4 Underspecified Interactions Between Service Provider and Service Discovery Entities. Among the service discovery systems that we analyzed, only one specified interactions between a service provider and a SDE. In this case, the specification defines an application-programming interface (API) that permits a service provider to interact with a local proxy the implements the functions of a SDE. The specification exhibits two limitations: (1) each SDE supports only a single service provider and (2) a cooperating service provider and SDE operate on the same node. Service discovery systems could be designed to support more flexible arrangements. For example, one SDE might proxy on behalf of multiple service providers or service providers might operate independently on separate nodes from a proxy SDE. Such arrangements would benefit from definition of protocol elements to allow a service provider to convey to a SDE the status and description of the associated service, to withdraw the service if necessary, and to ensure appropriate notification of failures between the service provider and SDE. Most of the service discovery systems we analyzed rely on proprietary APIs for interaction between a service provider and SDE. In these cases, the associated interactions fall outside the scope of the service discovery system. Based on this state of affairs, we opted to exclude from our model any description of interactions between service providers and SDEs.

3.6.5 Insufficient Specification of Relationship between Service Description and Eventable Variables. Though one of the service discovery systems that we analyzed includes eventable variables within its scope, no system that we analyzed provided a clear specification of the relationship between service descriptions and eventable service variables. All of the specifications we analyzed included a concept of service attributes, often expressed as a list of keyword-value pairs intended to describe the essential characteristics of a service. Typically, service attributes appear intended to change infrequently. For example, the resolution of a printer would not usually change without a hardware alteration and a software driver update. On the other hand, a service description could include attributes that change more frequently. For example, the number of jobs queued at a printer would fluctuate with demand. Most service discovery systems we analyzed do not distinguish among attributes based on likely update frequency. Lacking such a distinction, the same update procedures must be applied whenever a service attribute changes, no matter how frequently. Some service discovery systems only support updating of service descriptions through complete overwriting, while some systems support partial updating of only selected attribute values. No matter how service descriptions might be updated, all the service discovery systems that we analyzed permit a client to register for notification about any of multiple changes to a service description; however, resulting notifications do not necessarily detail the changes. This implies that, upon learning of a change, a client might need to retrieve a current copy of a service description and then compare it to a previously cached copy in order to determine the precise nature of any changes.

Unfortunately, the one specification we analyzed that did include eventable variables only indicated the existence of such variables in its service descriptions; the variables themselves are supplied directly by a service provider. Upon learning about the existence of eventable variables, a client needs to subscribe with the service provider to receive any related events. The specification does not include the concept of repositories, and thus does not specify procedures for a service provider to relay (to a repository) any changes in eventable variables. Further, the specification: (1) does not define what constitutes a significant change (and thus warrants sending an event) and (2) does not include mechanisms for rate control to ensure receivers do not emit events at unsustainable rates.

For these reasons, our model allows eventable variables to be included optionally in a service description (recall `ServiceVariableDescription` in Figure 3-1) and to be provided optionally by a service provider (recall `ServiceVariableDescription` in Figure 3-13). Further, our model allows a service provider to update eventable variables stored in a service description on a repository (see Section 3.4.2.1) as well as to update such variables directly within the service provider (see Section 3.5). Our model neither defines nor constrains how these mechanisms may be used to indicate the transient state of eventable variables. Our model also does not define what constitutes a significant event and does not include any mechanisms to control the rate at which events may be generated.

3.6.6 Failure to Consider Resource-Constrained Devices. None of the service discovery systems that we analyzed makes specific accommodations for resource-constrained devices. In fact, all assume availability of Internet networking software and consider system devices to be of fairly equal capability, at the level of a desktop or notebook computer. For these reasons, our model defines components that may be deployed on any device within a service discovery system. We can easily imagine resource-constrained devices incapable of hosting such components. Some researchers [e.g., 33] are investigating designs that explicitly accommodate variation in the capability of devices within a service discovery system.

4. Performance Considerations.

Service discovery protocols must work in environments of uncertain scale, which can present performance difficulties under some conditions. Most of the first-generation service discovery systems that we analyzed did not address such design considerations, instead leaving it to implementers to identify potential problems and provide suitable solutions. To guide implementers, we identify three classes of performance problems that could arise in deployments of service discovery systems, and we propose some solutions that might be adopted. One type of performance problem arises from the potential for multicast response implosion, which can occur whenever an unexpectedly large number of respondents inundate the issuer of a multicast query with too many messages. A second type of performance problem can occur when registrants overwhelm a registry with extension requests arriving too frequently. A third type of performance problem can appear when a large number of polling clients target an inappropriate subset of available repository replicas. Below, we discuss each of these performance issues and possible solutions, and we describe how our model accommodates the various solutions that we suggest.

4.1 Multicast Implosion Avoidance. All of the service discovery systems that we analyzed permit a component to issue multicast queries into networks with an unknown population of potential respondents. This could lead to response implosion, where a large number of replies descend on the query issuer. To mitigate response implosion, our model allows multicast queries to include an optional list of already discovered entities. This eliminates the need for known respondents to issue duplicate replies. Of course, a first query, which includes an empty list of previous responders, could still elicit a response implosion. Our model includes some optional algorithms to spread responses to multicast queries over a period of time. One class of algorithm requires potential respondents to reply only with some probability. A second class of algorithm requires potential respondents to compute a time to respond. In describing the various algorithms, we use some variables, listed and defined in Table 4-1, which also shows how the variables map to our UML model.

4.1.1 Probabilistic Response. One strategy to dampen multicast response implosion is to ensure that only a subset of potential respondents reply to a given query. On the surface, this strategy appears to reduce the likelihood of discovering all available components; however, if multicast queries are issued repeatedly over some time period, then the probability of discovering each component increases with time. To support a probabilistic response strategy, our model allows cyclic multicast queries (recall Section 3.2.2), where each query could include a parameter, M, denoting the number of queries that compose the cycle. Upon receiving a query message, each potential respondent can check the previous-responders list (if present), and then, if not on the list, the respondent can send a reply with probability $1/M$. Figure 4-1 illustrates the operation of this algorithm when a seeker of some discoverable items sends a multicast probe to a set of advertisers.

This algorithm would tend to reduce the volume of the response implosion; however, two problems remain. First, since replies are probabilistic, some potential respondents might not be discovered (though persistent recurrence of multicast queries will ultimately overcome this). Second, if M is small with respect to the population, P, of potential respondents, then the number of respondents to any particular multicast query could still prove quite large. To overcome these issues, we observe that the population of potential respondents is likely to have been observing multicast network traffic (e.g., probes and announcements) for a period of time. Given this, each potential respondent, i, likely has an estimate, P_i, of the population. When P_i is significantly larger than M, a potential respondent could choose to respond with probability $1/P_i$ instead of $1/M$. Further, response messages could convey P_i; thus, allowing the query issuer to receive estimates of population size, which could be used to determine the number of multicast queries to issue (and a better choice for M), to estimate memory requirements for a receiver's cache, and to decide when a multicast query issuer has discovered all members of the population. Figure 4-2 illustrates the operation of this algorithm in a context comparable to that of Figure 4-1.

Table 4-1. Key Variables Used in Multicast Implosion Avoidance Algorithms

Variable	UML Model Designation		Definition
	Class	Attributeor Method	
M	Advertiser	expectedNumberOfProbes parameter in aggressiveProbe()	Number of messages in a multicast announcement cycle
P_i	MulticastResponseSuppression	populationEstimate	Number of potential respondents, as estimated by advertiser i
L	ResponseUpperBound	getUpperBound()	The time limit after which potential respondents should not respond
R	ResponseRate	getResponseRate()	Rate (messages/sec) at which a respondent should send responses
A_i	MulticastResponseScheduling	numRespWithLowerAddress	Number of potential respondents with a lower address, as estimated by advertiser i
N_i	MulticastResponseScheduling	averageNumMsgsPerRespondent	Average number of messages per potential respondent, as estimated by advertiser i
X_i	MulticastResponseScheduling	averageResponseRate	Average response rate (messages/sec) per potential respondent, as estimated by advertiser i
T_i	MulticastResponseScheduling	getResponseTime()	Time for advertiser i to respond
A_n	RespondentEstimate	RespondentAddress	Address for potential respondent n
N_n	RespondentEstimate	numMsgsForRespondent	Estimated number of messages for respondent n
X_n	RespondentEstimate	estimatedResponseRate	Estimated response rate (messages/sec) for respondent n

To support a multicast-response suppression strategy, we augment our model as shown in Figure 4-3. (Table 4-1 shows the mapping between variables in our multicast-response implosion avoidance algorithms and elements of our UML model of service discovery systems.) First, we include an optional `ReplySuppressionParameter` (this is M) as part of configuring a `SeekerProxy`. Second, we include an optional `PopulationEstimate` (this is P_i) as part of configuring an advertiser. We also extend the `<<remote>>` method `Advertiser.aggressiveProbe()` to convey the `ReplySuppressionParameter` from the `SeekerProxy`. Finally, we extend the <<remote>> method `SeekerProxy.aggressiveResponse()` to accept the `PopuluationEstimate` from each advertiser.

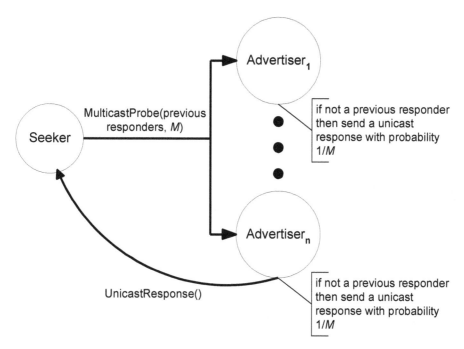

Probabilistic Response without Population Estimation

Figure 4-1. Using Probabilistic Response to Combat Response Implosion

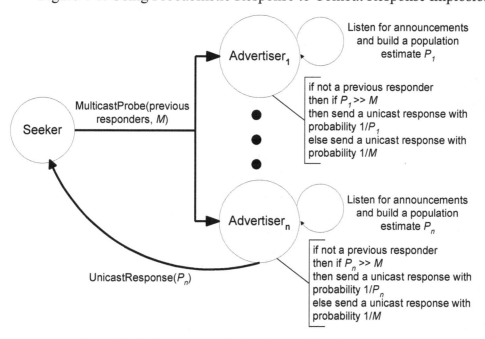

Probabilistic Response with Population Estimation

Figure 4-2. Using Probabilistic Response with Population Estimation to Combat Response Implosion

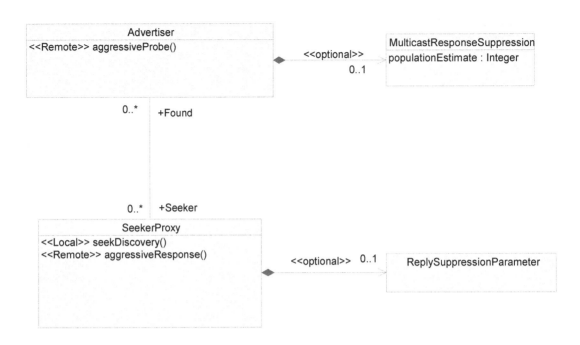

Figure 4-3. Class Diagram augmentations Supporting Multicast-response Suppression

4.1.2 Timed Response. As an alternative (or supplement) to multicast-response suppression, our model permits some optional algorithms for multicast-response scheduling. Here, the goal is to allow all potential respondents to reply to any given multicast query, but in a form that limits response implosion. Our optional algorithms have two dimensions: (1) when to reply (*random* or *scheduled*) and (2) how fast to reply (*burst* or *paced*). The dimensions can be combined to support four possible response strategies: (1) random burst (RB), (2) random paced (RP), (3) scheduled burst (SB), or (4) scheduled paced (SP). To accommodate these strategies, we augmented our model with some additional classes and associations, as shown in Figure 4-4.

4.1.2.1 Random Response Strategy. When supporting a random-response strategy, each multicast query includes a time limit, L, and each respondent selects a random time, uniformly distributed over $0\dots L$, to issue its response messages (see Figure 4-5). Where a respondent issues more than one message in response to a query, which can occur in selected service discovery protocols, the messages may be sent (for the random burst strategy) as fast as possible, or (for the random paced strategy) at a rate, R, conveyed in the multicast query (see Figure 4-6). Including R in each multicast query allows a query issuer to denote the rate (in messages per second) at which replies can be consumed. In Figure 4-4, the method `getUpperBound()` in the optional class `ResponseUpperBound` is used to obtain a value for L, which is conveyed in invocations of `<<remote>>` method `Advertiser.aggressiveProbe()`. When response messages are to be paced, the rate parameter (R) is also conveyed in invocations of `aggressiveProbe()`.

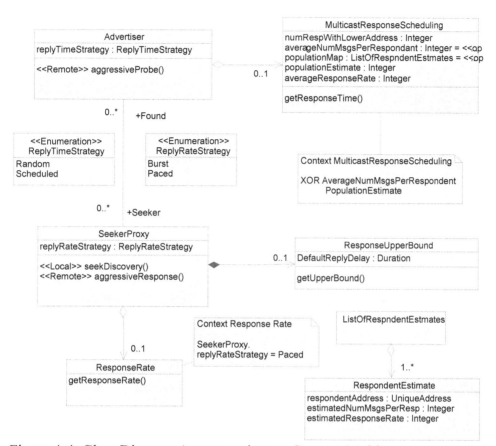

Figure 4-4. Class Diagram Augmentations to Support Multicast-response Scheduling

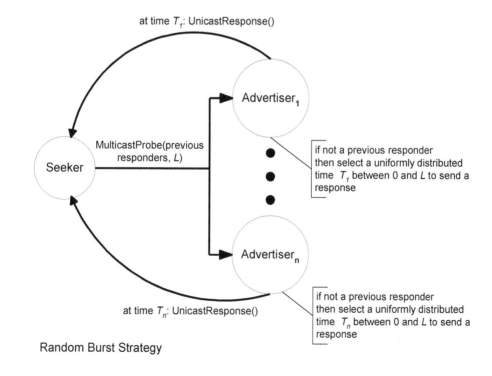

Figure 4-5. Using a Random-Burst Algorithm to Combat Response Implosion

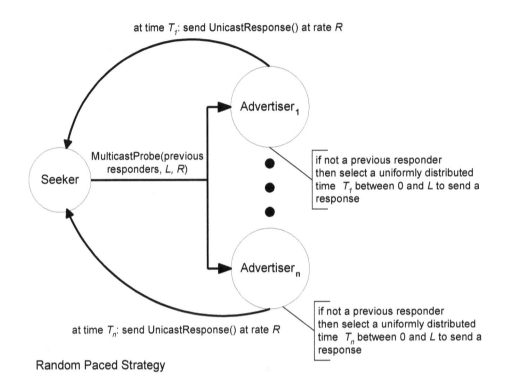

Figure 4-6. Using a Random-Paced Algorithm to Combat Response Implosion

4.1.2.2 Scheduled Response Strategy. In a scheduled response strategy, each potential respondent computes a time to send response messages. The goal is to compute a time different from other potential respondents. Using a scheduled response strategy relies on each potential respondent, i, to observe multicast traffic for a period of time and develop some estimate, A_i, of the number of potential respondents with a lower address. Further, each potential respondent must form an estimate, N_i, of the average number of response messages to be sent by a population member. Assuming that potential respondents reply in ascending address order and that respondents send response messages at some estimated pace, X_i, then given N_i, X_i, A_i, a respondent can select a time, T_i, to respond, where $T_i = A_i (N_i/X_i)$. Note that a vector of estimates can replace the averages N_i and X_i for each potential respondent. For example, if S is the set of respondents with a lower address than potential respondent i, then $T_i = \sum_{n=1}^{|S|} (N_n / X_n)$, where n denotes a respondent in the set S, N_n denotes the number of response messages expected to be sent by respondent n and X_n denotes the rate at which respondent n is expected to send messages. Using a vector provides a more accurate T_i at the cost of additional memory and computation. Regardless of how T_i is computed, if $T_i > L$, then the potential respondent should not respond, because the scheduled response would occur after the time limit included in the multicast query. If $T_i \leq L$, then the potential respondent should send any response messages starting at time T_i. If a scheduled burst policy (see Figure 4-7) is in effect, then the messages should be sent as fast as possible; however, if a scheduled paced policy (see Figure 4-8) is in effect, then the messages should be sent at rate R, as specified in the query message, and $X_i = R$ (for the average case) or $X_n = R$ (for the vector case) should be used when computing T_i. Given that each respondent has a population estimate, P_i, each response message should include P_i, so that the query issuer can consider a new value for L, which could allow a longer period over which to receive query replies. Elsewhere [22], we outline the performance of the four algorithms for multicast response scheduling, as applied to a specific service discovery protocol.

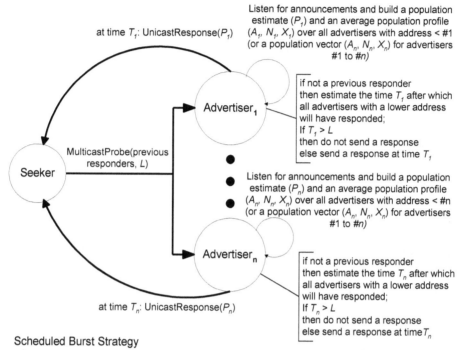

Figure 4-7. Using a Scheduled-Burst Algorithm to Combat Response Implosion.

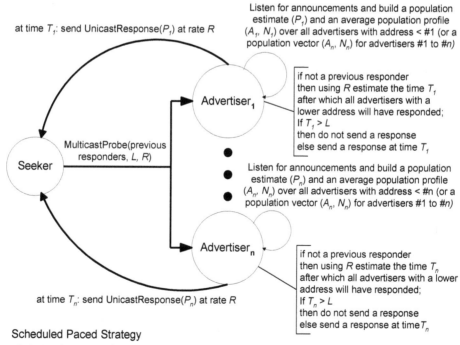

Figure 4-8. Using a Scheduled-Paced Algorithm to Combat Response Implosion

To support a scheduled response strategy, we augment our model (recall Figure 4-4) to associate an optional class, `MulticastResponseScheduling`, with advertisers. The class includes a method, `getResponseTime()`, to compute a T_i for the associated advertiser. To support computation of T_i based on averages, the optional class includes parameters: `NumRespWithLowerAddress` (A_i), `AverageResponseRate` (X_i), and `AverageNumMsgsPerRespondent` (N_i). To support computation of T_i based on a vector, the optional class includes a population map that represents the address of, and the estimated number of messages to be sent by, each known potential respondent. The population map should be maintained in increasing order of respondent address. The optional class also includes a population estimate (P_i) that is conveyed back to the query source in invocations of the `<<remote>>` method `aggressiveResponse()`.

4.2 Extension Policy. Many service discovery systems support the concept of registries that can accept registrations of service descriptions and, possibly, notification requests. Typically, to maintain registration beyond an initial granted period, registrants must contact registries periodically. Usually, registries have a maximum capacity (based on available storage space) to accept registrations, and may need to limit the capacity (based on available processor time) to process renewal requests. Renewal processing limits have performance implications, which we explore here. Our discussion refers to some variables, listed and defined in Table 4-2, which also shows the mapping of the variables to elements of the UML model.

Table 4-2. Key Variables Used in Various Extension Algorithms

Variable	UML Model Designation		Definition
	Class	**Attribute or Method**	
C	`ExtensionGranter`	`maxExtensionsPerSecond`	Maximum number of extensions/sec that an extension granter can process
N	`Registry`	`registrations-> count(Registration)`	Count of registrations currently maintained by a registry
H_{MIN}	`ExtensionGranter`	`minimumTTL`	Minimum extension that an extension granter may assign
H_{MAX}	`ExtensionGranter`	`maximumTTL`	Maximum extension that an extension granter may assign
H	`FixedExtensionGranter`	`fixedTTL`	Extension assigned by an extension granter using fixed-assignment
N_{MAX}	`FixedExtensionGranter` `RandomExtensionGranter`	`maxNumberExtensionsAllowed`	Maximum number of extensions that may be granted by an extension granter using fixed-or random-assignment
H_Q	`RequestedExtensionGranter`	`refresh()`	An extension duration requested when using requested assignment
H_R	`RequestedExtensionGranter`	`getTTL()`	An extension duration granted when using requested assignment
H_A	`AdaptiveExtensionGranter`	`getTTL()`	An extension duration granted when using adaptive assignment
P_C	`PriorityExtensionGranter`	`nukmberOfPriorityClasses`	Number of priority classes supported under priority assignment
P_S	`PriorityExtensionGranter`	`prioritySlotSize`	Duration that may be assigned for each priority slot under priority assignment
P_R	`PriorityExtensionGranter`	`refresh()`	Requested priority when requesting an extension under priority assignment
H_P	`PriorityExtensionGranter`	`getTTL()`	An extension duration granted when using priority assignment

Assume each request requires P seconds to process. If unbounded, then the amount of processing time (T) devoted to renewal requests would grow with the number of registrations, N, according to $T = N \cdot P$. In general, the platform hosting a registry may also host other services that require processor time; thus, it seems likely that the platform would desire to limit the amount of processor time available to each of its services. For this reason, we assume that a platform hosting a registry will define a maximum capacity, C renewals per second, to devote to processing renewal requests. This suggests that to accommodate a growing population of registrations, while respecting the available capacity, the time between renewals must increase. In general, given N registrations that can be renewed at rate C, then the period between renewals, H, must be $H = N/C$. When a renewal is requested, some means must exist for the extension granter to select a time-to-live (TTL) value to assign to the extension. One could simply assign H as the TTL; however, as N increases the value of H increases, which has implications for failure-detection latency (i.e., the delay between failure of a component and detection of the failure by other components). Assuming uniformly distributed failure times and an average TTL value, H_{TTL}, failure-detection latency will be $H_{TTL}/2$ on average. Assigning higher TTL values, leads to higher failure-detection latency, while assigning lower TTL values, leads to lower failure-detection latency. A given extension granter may wish to limit failure-detection latency, which implies that H must not exceed an upper bound, H_{MAX}, and thus, since C is fixed, there must be an upper bound, N_{MAX}, on the number of registrants. Further, if an extension granter assigns small TTL values, then the extension requester could be required to renew quite frequently, which might place an excessive renewal load on platforms hosting extension requesters. For this reason, one could place a lower bound, H_{MIN}, on granted TTLs. Given these factors, one could devise numerous policies for assigning TTL values. Here, we describe five.

Figure 4-9 shows a class diagram augmented to support the optional extension policies that we include in our model. (Table 4-2 relates elements from Figure 4-9 to variables used in the extension algorithms we explain below.) We augment the abstract class `ExtensionGranter` to include attributes: `maxExtensionsPerSecond` (C), `minimumTTL` (H_{MIN}), and `maximumTTL` (H_{MAX}). We assume that the current number of registrations, N, can be determined by consulting the set of registrations maintained by the associated registry. To determine a TTL value (H), the `ExtensionGranter` class provides a method, `getTTL()`, which must be overridden by specializations. `ExtensionGranter` can be specialized to employ one of five TTL assignment polices (Fixed, Random, Requested, Adaptive, or Priority). Some specializations also include additional attributes to support the algorithm encapsulated in the `getTTL()` method. Below, we discuss each assignment policy in turn.

4.2.1 Fixed Assignment. In a fixed-assignment scheme (see Figure 4-9, `FixedExtensionGranter`) each request for extension is given a fixed TTL value, H (`fixedTTL`), to derive a maximum number (`maxNumberExtensionsAllowed`), $N_{MAX} = C \cdot H$, of extensions that can be granted. The value chosen for H must fall between the inherited (or overridden) minimum, H_{MIN}, and maximum, H_{MAX}, TTL values that may be granted. An extension granter must deny any request for an extension that would cause

N_{MAX} to be exceeded. The scheme, illustrated in Figure 4-10, leads to a fixed failure-detection latency, and presents a known workload to extension requesters.

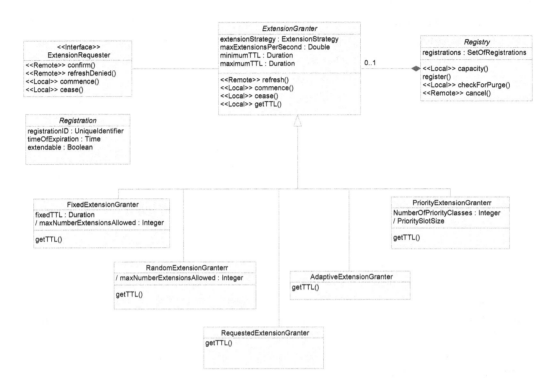

Figure 4- 9. Class Diagram Augmented to Support Optional Extension Polices

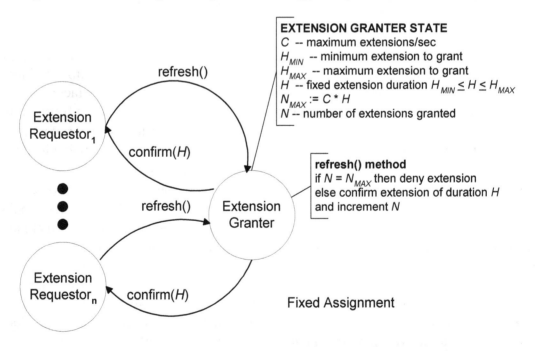

Figure 4-10. Using a Fixed-Assignment Algorithm to Grant Extensions.

4.2.2 Random Assignment. In a random-assignment scheme, (see Figure 4-9, `RandomExtensionGranter`) each extension request is assigned a TTL value, H, which is selected randomly from a uniform distribution ranging over H_{MIN} to H_{MAX}. The extension granter must deny requests for an extension whenever granting the request would exceed the derived attributed (`maxNumberExtensionsAllowed`) $N_{MAX} = C (H_{MIN} + H_{MAX})/2$. This scheme, illustrated in Figure 4-11, causes extension requesters to receive varying levels of failure-detection latency, and presents a variable workload to extension requesters.

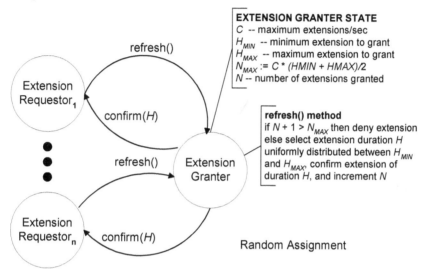

Figure 4-11. Using a Random-Assignment Algorithm to Grant Extensions.

4.2.3 Requested Assignment. In a requested-assignment scheme, (see Figure 4-9, `RequestedExtensionGranter`) each extension request includes a requested TTL value, H_Q. If $H_{MIN} \leq H_Q \leq H_{MAX}$, then the extension granter assigns a TTL, $H_R = H_Q$. If $H_Q < H_{MIN}$, then the extension granter assigns a TTL, $H_R = H_{MIN}$. If $H_{MAX} < H_Q$, then the extension granter assigns a TTL, $H_R = H_{MAX}$. The extension granter must tally the current number, N, of granted extensions and the sum, H_{SUM}, over all assigned TTL values, i.e., $H_{SUM} = \sum_{i=1}^{N} (H_R)_i$. The extension granter must deny requests for an extension whenever granting the request would lead to $N/H_{SUM} > C$. This scheme, illustrated in Figure 4-12, allows extension requesters to receive the requested TTL, as long as the request falls within the permitted bounds.

4.2.4 Adaptive Assignment. In an adaptive-assignment scheme, the extension granter (see Figure 4-9, `AdaptiveExtensionGranter`) must use the current number, N, of granted extensions to assign a TTL, $H_A = N/C$. If the assigned TTL exceeds the maximum (i.e., $H_A > H_{MAX}$), then the extension request must be denied. If the assigned TTL falls below the minimum (i.e., $H_A < H_{MIN}$), then the minimum TTL is assigned (i.e., $H_A = H_{MIN}$). This scheme, illustrated in Figure 4-13, ensures the extension requester will receive the lowest possible TTL, given the current number of granted extensions and a maximum capacity to process extensions; thus, the failure-detection latency is maintained at the lowest possible level, at the cost of increasing workload for extension requesters.

Elsewhere [23], we report on the performance of this versatile adaptive-assignment algorithm when applied in various service discovery systems.

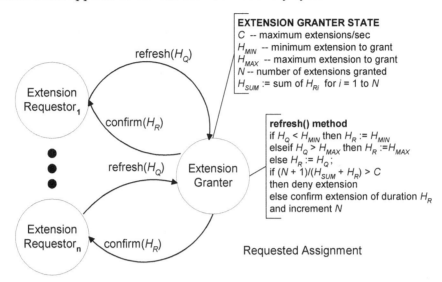

Figure 4-12. Using a Requested-Assignment Algorithm to Grant Extensions.

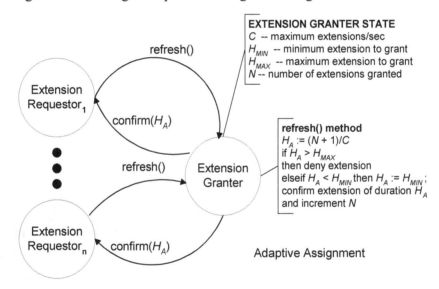

Figure 4-13. Using an Adaptive-Assignment Algorithm to Grant Extensions.

4.2.5 Priority Assignment. In a priority-assignment scheme, (see Figure 4-9, `PriorityExtensionGranter`) extension requesters can be classified according to their priority with respect to failure-detection latency, allowing those in need of lower failure-detection latencies to receive lower TTL values, while those with less stringent requirements may receive higher TTL values. The priority-assignment scheme requires one additional parameter (`NumberOfPriorityClasses`): the number, P_C, of priority classes, which permits calculation of a priority slot size (`PrioritySlotSize`), $P_S = (H_{MAX} - H_{MIN})/(P_C - 1)$. Each extension request includes a requested priority, P_R, such that $0 \leq P_R < P_C$. The extension granter assigns a TTL value, $H_P = H_{MIN} + (P_S) P_R$. The extension granter must tally the current number, N, of granted extensions and the sum, H_{SUM}, over all assigned TTL values, i.e., $H_{SUM} = \sum_{i=1}^{N} (H_P)_i$. The extension granter must deny requests for an extension whenever granting the request would lead to $N/H_{SUM} > C$.

The first-come, first-served nature of this scheme, illustrated in Figure 4-14, could permit starvation among various priority classes depending upon the order in which extension requests arrive. For example, given a sufficient number of requests for lower priority extensions (i.e., those with higher priority class numbers), a later extension request with higher priority could be denied because no capacity remains. To circumvent possible starvation, we recommend assigning separate capacity, C_P, to each priority class, and then tracking utilization separately for each priority class. Alternatively, separate capacity could be allocated for each priority class, and any one of the other assignment schemes could be used for each of the priority classes. More sophisticated schemes seem possible. For example, capacity may be shared among all priority classes, but then reclaimed as necessary to support the demands of higher priority classes. We leave these more sophisticated schemes, which could require small changes to our model, for future work.

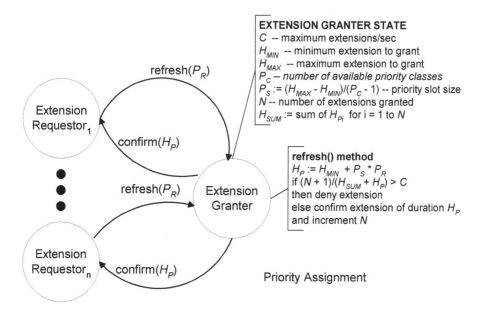

EXTENSION GRANTER STATE
C -- maximum extensions/sec
H_{MIN} -- minimum extension to grant
H_{MAX} -- maximum extension to grant
P_C -- number of available priority classes
$P_S := (H_{MAX} - H_{MIN})/(P_C - 1)$ -- priority slot size
N -- number of extensions granted
$H_{SUM} :=$ sum of H_{Pi} for i = 1 to N

refresh() method
$H_P := H_{MIN} + P_S * P_R$
if $(N + 1)/(H_{SUM} + H_P) > C$
then deny extension
else confirm extension of duration H_P
and increment N

Priority Assignment

Figure 4-14. Using the Priority-Assignment Algorithm to Grant Extensions.

4.3 Replica Selection. Most of the service discovery systems we analyzed allow multiple repository replicas to exist, so that clients and services can still rendezvous when component failures prevent access to a given repository. The service discovery systems that we analyzed create replicas by requiring services to discover and register with all repositories found to have administrative scopes that intersect with those of the service. Given a set of replicated repositories, clients are free to query any discovered repository because all repositories with intersecting scopes should have similar information. This repository replication arrangement implies that clients could discover several replicas in a given scope, and then choose one of the replicas against which to issue any given query. This approach could be particularly useful in service discovery systems that do not support notification, but that instead require clients to periodically poll repositories to learn about service arrivals and departures, and about changes to service descriptions.

Given a population C of clients and R of repository replicas, where each client intends to issue repeated queries to poll repositories, a means must exist for each client to select a replica as target for each query. Absent any additional information, each client should probably select one of the replicas randomly with a uniform distribution. Random selection will spread the workload across the set of replicas, and should also provide similar average response time for each client. Unfortunately, each replica may be hosted on a computer platform of differing capacity and with time-varying background workload. For this reason, random query selection might not provide the best overall performance. On the other hand, since repositories in discovery systems periodically announce their status, one can imagine exploiting those announcements to transmit information about the varying capacity and current workload of each repository.

We define a query processing rate, G, to represent the capacity (in queries per second) of a repository to process queries. The value of G, which may vary over time, depends on the fixed processing rate of the computer executing the repository code and the size of the most likely path through that code, as well as on the varying percentage of the fixed processing rate that a computer can devote to processing repository queries. For example, imagine a system administrator assigns a minimum, G_{MIN}, and maximum, G_{MAX}, rate for processing repository queries. One can envision that a lightly loaded computer might be able to process G_{MAX} queries per second. As the computer becomes more heavily loaded, a smaller proportion of processing cycles can be devoted to handle repository queries, and so the transaction rate decreases ($G < G_{MAX}$). When the computer becomes even more loaded, then the transaction rate to process repository queries decreases toward $G = G_{MIN}$. As computational resources again become available, then the query processing rate can increase toward $G = G_{MAX}$. Variation in the value of G can affect the number, N, of backlogged queries waiting to be processed, and can also cause variation in the response times (N/G) provided by a given repository. Variation in the number of queries sent to a repository will also affect the value of N. The goal of a replica-selection algorithm is to direct queries to replicas in a fashion that will provide clients with the best response times and that will not cause repositories to become overloaded with queries.

In what follows, we describe five decentralized algorithms a client could use to select a target replica to query. Each algorithm (see Table 4-3 for definitions of key algorithm variables) assumes that repositories include in their announcements the following two parameters: (1) the number, N, of backlogged queries waiting to be processed and (2) the rate, G, at which the repository can currently process queries. (One could select alternate measures, such as the number of queries that arrived and the number of queries that departed since the previous announcement.) We assume that N and G represent instantaneous values at the time of the announcement; however, one could substitute alternate formulations, such as averages over the interval since the previous announcement. Given values N and G for a specific repository, r, i.e., N_r and G_r, a client can readily estimate the time required, $T_{Qr} = N_r/G_r$, for the repository to clear its backlog of queries. T_{Qr} estimates the latency before repository r begins to process a new query from a client. We define a bound, T_{QMAX}, such that a repository is considered overloaded when $T_{Qr} > T_{QMAX}$.

Table 4-3. Key Variables Used in Various Replica-Selection Algorithms

Variable	UML Model Designation		Definition
	Class	Attributeor Method	
N_r	`SeekerProxy`	`aggressiveResponse()` `directedResponse()` `lazyAnnouncement()`	Current number of queries waiting at repository r
G_r	`SeekerProxy`	`aggressiveResponse()` `directedResponse()` `lazyAnnouncement()`	Current rate at which repository r can process queries
T_{Qr}	`UnicastServiceSeeker`	`knownRepositories`	Estimated latency (N_r/G_r) for repository r to clear its backlog of queries
T_{QMAX}	`Overload`	`limit`	A repository r is considered overloaded if $T_{Qr} > T_{QMAX}$
P_r	`WeightedSchemePoller` `BalancedSchemePoller`	`selectRepository()`	Probability of selecting repository r
T_{QREF}	`BalancedSchemePoller`	`knownRepositories`	A target value for repository latency, selected as the maximum T_{Qr} over all repositories
N_{Dr}	`BalancedSchemePoller`	`selectRepository()`	Number of queries required for the latency of repository r to reach T_{QREF}

Figure 4-15 shows a class diagram augmented to support the optional replica-selection algorithms that we include in our model. We define two optional element-value pairs, `NumberQueriesPending` and `CurrentQueryProcessingRate`, to represent, respectively, the number of backlogged queries (N_r) and the current query-processing rate (G_r) associated with a repository (r). When supporting one of our optional replica selection algorithms, repositories must include the current values of these two optional elements in each announcement message. We add `<<local>>` method, `selectRepository()` to the class `UnicastServiceSeeker`. This default method returns one repository, selected randomly (using a uniform distribution) from the set R of known repositories (see Figure 4-16). To implement one of our optional replica selection algorithms, the `UnicastServiceSeeker` class must be specialized, so that the default method `selectRepository()` can be overridden appropriately, to implement the desired selection scheme (greedy, partition, weighted, balanced, or balanced partition). Elsewhere [24], we provide detailed simulation results highlighting relative performance differences among these algorithms. Below, we explain the algorithms.

4.3.1 Greedy Scheme. In a greedy scheme (Figure 4-15 `GreedySchemePoller`), each client computes T_Q for each repository and then queries the repository with the lowest T_Q. In simulation experiments with this scheme, which causes all clients to descend on the repository promising lowest delay, we find that average system response time improves significantly when compared with random selection. In addition, when compared with random selection, the greedy algorithm, illustrated in Figure 4-17, results in a significantly lower overload rate among repositories. On the other hand, the oscillatory nature of the greedy scheme causes repositories to exhibit significantly higher variance in response time, as compared with random selection.

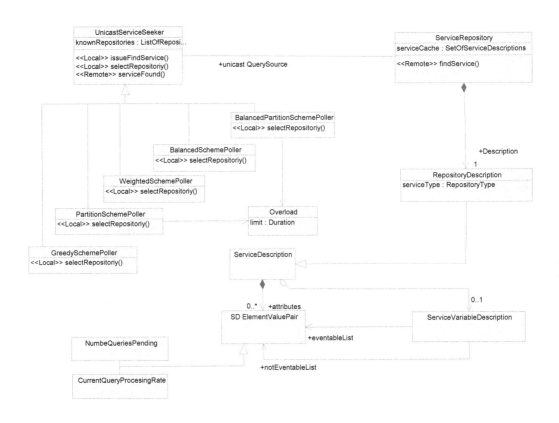

Figure 4-15. Class Diagram Augmented to Support Optional Replica Selection Algorithms

4.3.2 Partition Scheme. In a partition scheme (Figure 4-15 `ClassSchemePoller`), each client computes T_Q for each repository and then partitions repositories into two classes (e.g., available or overloaded) based on whether $T_Q < T_{QMAX}$. Each client then randomly chooses a repository to query from among the available class. In simulation experiments, the partition scheme yields significantly lower response time and overload rate (and also reduced variance), when compared against the greedy and random schemes. The partition scheme, illustrated in Figure 4-18, does, however, exhibit some behavioral issues. For example, as total system workload increases, repositories slowly migrate toward the overloaded class, leaving clients fewer repositories to target in the available class. As repositories in the overloaded class reduce the backlog of work and became more lightly loaded, clients learn of these changes only when receiving new announcements. This delay in information dissemination leads to periods of underutilization ($T_Q = 0$) for repositories. Further, while the overall system workload remains constant, the number of available repositories oscillates, which leads to periods when the few available repositories are more likely to become overloaded.

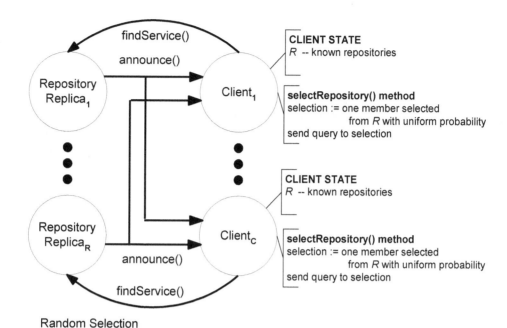

Figure 4-16. Using Random Selection to Identify a Replica to Query.

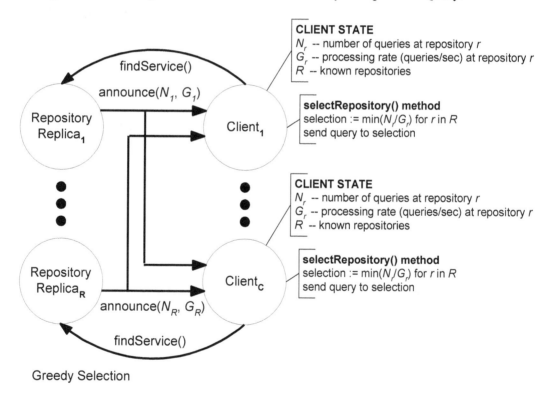

Figure 4-17. Using a Greedy Algorithm to Select a Replica to Query.

4.3.3 Weighted Scheme. In a weighted scheme (WeightedSchemePoller in Figure 4-15), each client computes T_{Qr} for each repository (i.e., T_{Qr} is T_Q for repository r) and then assigns a repository weight ($1/T_{Qr}$). The client then sums the weights for all repositories (the set R) and divides each individual weight by the sum to assign a probability, $P_r = (1/T_{Qr})/\sum_{i=1}^{|R|} 1/T_{Qi})$, proportional to the weight. These probabilities are arranged in a distribution dividing the unit interval. The client then selects a uniformly distributed random fraction (between 0 and 1) to index the probability distribution, selecting one repository to query. Simulation experiments with this weighted scheme, which causes repositories to receive queries based on their estimated processing latencies, gives substantially lower response time, overload rate, and variance, when compared with the partition scheme. The weighted scheme, illustrated in Figure 4-19, does, however, exhibit one shortcoming. Since T_Q is computed as N/G, repositories can show similar values of T_Q even though some repositories have a larger capacity (G) than others. The weighted scheme directs a similar number of queries to repositories with similar T_Q values, even though some repositories may have the capacity to process many more queries per second than others.

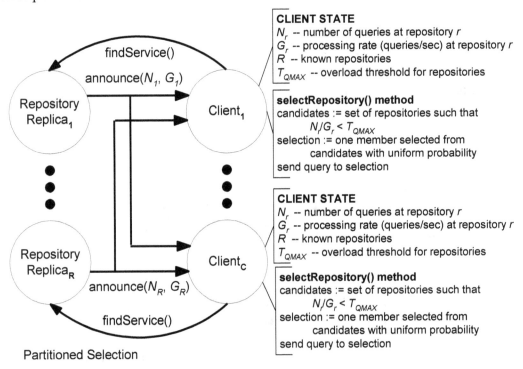

Figure 4-18. Using a Partition Algorithm to Select a Replica to Query.

4.3.4 Balanced Scheme. In a balanced scheme (`BalancedSchemePoller` in Figure 4-15), each client computes $T_{Qr} = N_r/G_r$ for each repository, and selects the largest as a reference value, T_{QREF}. Each client then determines the number, N_{Dr}, of queries that must be added to each repository in order to match the reference value, i.e., $N_{Dr} = G_r (T_{QREF}) - N_r$. The client uses N_{Dr} to compute a probability, $P_r = N_{Dr} / \sum_{i=1}^{|R|} N_{Di}$, for each repository (in the set R of known repositories), and arranges the probabilities in a distribution apportioning the unit interval. The client then selects a uniformly distributed random fraction (between 0 and 1) to index the probability distribution, selecting one repository to query. Simulation experiments reveal that the balanced scheme yields significantly lower response time, overload rate, and variance then the weighted scheme. The balanced scheme, illustrated in Figure 4-20, exhibits stable behavior because queries are directed toward repositories based on ability to absorb them. The algorithm does, however, allow overloaded repositories ($T_{Qr} > T_{QMAX}$) to receive queries because T_{QREF} might exceed T_{QMAX}.

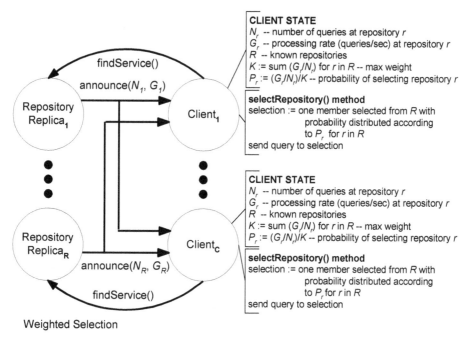

CLIENT STATE
N_r -- number of queries at repository r
G_r -- processing rate (queries/sec) at repository r
R -- known repositories
K := sum (G_r/N_r) for r in R -- max weight
P_r := $(G_r/N_r)/K$ -- probability of selecting repository r

selectRepository() method
selection := one member selected from R with
        probability distributed according
        to P_r for r in R
send query to selection

CLIENT STATE
N_r -- number of queries at repository r
G_r -- processing rate (queries/sec) at repository r
R -- known repositories
K := sum (G_r/N_r) for r in R -- max weight
P_r := $(G_r/N_r)/K$ -- probability of selecting repository r

selectRepository() method
selection := one member selected from R with
        probability distributed according
        to P_r for r in R
send query to selection

Figure 4-19. Using a Weighted Algorithm to Select a Replica to Query.

4.3.5 Balanced-Partition Scheme. In a balanced-partition scheme (Figure 4-15 `BalancedClassSchemePoller`), each client computes $T_{Qr} = N_r/G_r$ for each repository, and selects as a reference value the largest T_{Qr} below T_{QMAX}, i.e., $T_{QREF} = \max (T_{Qr}) < T_{QMAX}$. The client then partitions repositories into two classes: overloaded ($T_{Qr} \geq T_{QMAX}$) and available ($T_{Qr} < T_{QMAX}$) and applies the balanced scheme to all repositories in the available class. If the available class is empty, then the client applies the balanced scheme to repositories in the overloaded class. This balanced-partition scheme, illustrated in Figure 4-21, divides repositories into available and overloaded classes, and then directs queries effectively among repositories in the available class. When all repositories are overloaded, the balanced-partition scheme reverts to the balanced scheme. As system load increases, more repositories are pushed into the overloaded class; however, more capable repositories (with larger G_r) tend to remain longer in the available class, allowing system workload to be apportioned more effectively. Once all repositories become overloaded, system workload continues to be apportioned based on the ability of individual repositories to absorb queries. Simulation results show that the balanced algorithm outperforms the balanced-partition algorithm, because (prior to system overload) partitioning reduces the number of repositories to which queries may be assigned.

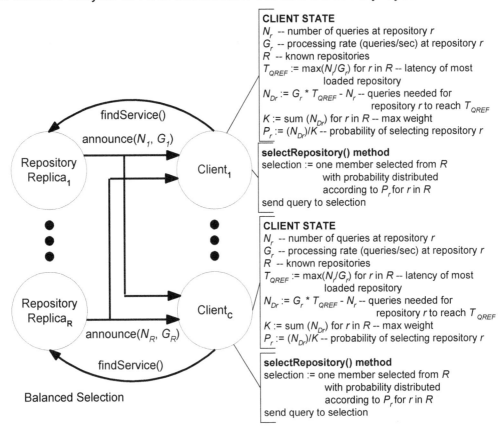

Figure 4-20. Using a Balanced Algorithm to Select a Replica to Query.

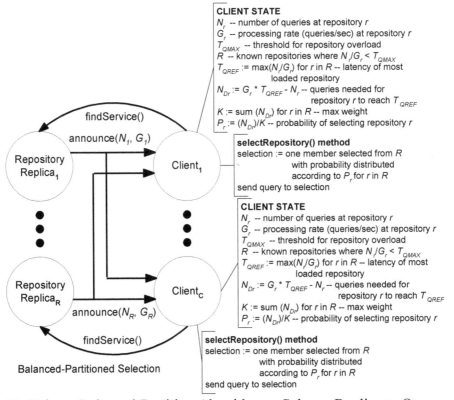

Figure 4-21. Using a Balanced-Partition Algorithm to Select a Replica to Query.

5. Service Guarantees

None of the first-generation discovery systems that we examined includes a definition of service guarantees. In this section, we exploit our model to define (both informally and formally) a set of qualified, service guarantees that we believe discovery systems should attempt to satisfy. We formulate each guarantee as a consistent state that a service discovery system should attempt to achieve. For example, new information should be conveyed to all participants, and all participants should purge stale information. We cannot formulate such guarantees without two qualifications. First, protocol designs, configuration parameters, and network delays typically introduce some latency before information can be propagated; thus, service discovery systems can exhibit inconsistent states, which should, however, be bounded in time. Further, service discovery systems operate in dynamic environments, where service availability may vary, where application needs may change, and where nodes and links may fail. Due to such uncertainties, the definition of consistent state changes over time as a service discovery system operates. Subject to these qualifications, we believe that discovery systems should seek to provide specified guarantees, as we define below. We also discuss the confounding influences that can delay or interfere with service guarantees.

We begin with an informal discussion of our proposed service guarantees. Broadly, we conceive service guarantees in four categories: (1) discovery guarantees, (2) registration guarantees, (3) update guarantees, and (4) discard guarantees. Discovery guarantees (Section 5.1) specify the conditions under which seekers should be able to obtain discoverable items they require. Registration guarantees (Section 5.2) specify the conditions under which information should be deposited successfully in a registry. Update guarantees (Section 5.3) specify the conditions under which participating entities should receive changes to existing discoverable items. Discard guarantees (Section 5.4) specify the conditions under which participating entities should discard discoveries.

After the informal discussion, we formalize (Section 5.5) our service guarantees as *consistency conditions*, that is, a set of consistent states that discovery systems should strive to achieve under specified circumstances. In general, we conceive our consistency conditions in the following form: while specified conditions (the *antecedent*) hold, then a particular consistent state (the *consequent*) should be achieved, eventually. We use the qualification of *eventually* because inconsistent states may exist temporarily as information dissemination incurs a propagation delay. Of course, the antecedent leading to the consequent might change during the time its takes to disseminate information; thus, the eventually clause is subject to a qualification that the antecedent must continue to hold during the transient period of inconsistency. If the antecedent fails to hold for a sufficient duration, then one should not expect the consequent to be achieved.

Formalizing our service guarantees enables us to represent them readily in computer programs. For example, we added our consistency conditions into simulation models [17-21] and used them to evaluate the ability of particular discovery systems to provide service guarantees. We have uncovered situations where a consistency condition remains unsatisfied for an unbounded time, indicating a likely design error in a service discovery system. We have also used our consistency conditions to measure the delay incurred in achieving consistent states. Further, we have used our consistency conditions to distinguish between latency associated with failure detection and latency due to failure restoration. Other researchers [34] have used our consistency conditions together with a model-checking program to verify a system design. These results indicate the value of formalizing service guarantees.

5.1 Kinds of Service Guarantees. Below, we provide a high-level description of the categories of service guarantees, which include Discovery, Registration, Update, and Discard guarantees.

5.1.1 Discovery Guarantees. The main goal of service discovery systems is to ensure that components become aware of information maintained by other components throughout a distributed system. In our model, this means that as new discoverable items become available, seekers of such items should be able to discover them. Our model supports discovery in two forms: *primary discovery* (using the discovery functions described in section 3.2) and *secondary discovery* (using the discovery functions described in section 3.4.1). We define a service guarantee for each form of discovery.

5.1.1.1 Primary Discovery. Primary discovery applies to items (i.e., administrative scopes, repository descriptions, service descriptions, and service types) that a seeker can discover directly. In general, an item is considered *discoverable* by a given seeker under the following conditions: (1) the seeker has a requirement for the item, (2) some advertiser is providing the item, (3) the seeker and advertiser can communicate through an active discovery function along an operational path, and (4) the seeker has not already found the item. Because a given seeker could potentially find multiple (m) instances of a discoverable item, our model allows a seeker to constrain the number (n) of discoverable items sought to satisfy a particular requirement. Given a set of m instances of some discoverable item and a seeker with a requirement for n instances of that item, a seeker should be guaranteed to discover the minimum of m or n instances of the discoverable item. We call this the *Primary Discovery* guarantee.

While a service discovery system should satisfy the *Primary Discovery* guarantee, a range of uncertainties can interfere. For example, information propagation may be delayed by network conditions (transmission delays and message loss) and by use of algorithms to avoid multicast-response implosion (as described in Section 4.1). In most situations, such factors cause a finite period of delay, during which the system is in an inconsistent state temporarily, but after which the *Primary Discovery* guarantee is achieved. In other circumstances, paths may transition between operational and non-operational states, affecting the ability of seekers and advertisers to communicate. If a path is not operational, the guarantee cannot be satisfied. Further, the number m of discoverable items can vary over time, and seekers may freely change the number n of discoverable items sought. For this reason, the *Primary Discovery* guarantee must be reconsidered with variations in n and m. Other factors may delay or prevent successful satisfaction of the *Primary Discovery* guarantee. For example, if various transmission intervals associated with discovery processes (i.e., lazy, aggressive, and directed) are configured to be too large, then discovery may be delayed beyond a useful time.

Similarly, discontinuing discovery processes prematurely can prevent discovery of some otherwise discoverable items.

5.1.1.2 Secondary Discovery. Secondary discovery applies only to (non-repository) service descriptions that a seeker may discover by querying a previously discovered repository. We assume that some seeker has acquired access (through primary discovery) to a repository, and aims to obtain service descriptions matching some requirement. In general, a service description is considered to be *retrievable* by a given seeker under the following conditions: (1) the seeker has a requirement for the service description, (2) the service description is contained in the repository, (3) the seeker and repository can communicate and a service retrieval process is active on an operational path, and (4) the seeker has not already retrieved the service description. Because a repository may contain multiple (m) retrievable service descriptions, our model allows a seeker to constrain the number (n) of service descriptions sought to satisfy a particular requirement. Given a set of m retrievable service descriptions and a seeker with a requirement for n instances of such descriptions, a seeker should be guaranteed to retrieve the minimum of m or n service descriptions from the repository. We call this the *Secondary Discovery* guarantee.

The *Secondary Discovery* guarantee is subject to the same qualifications as the *Primary Discovery* guarantee. One additional factor arises, however, because our model assumes that a path is either operational or not, whereas real communications paths can operate temporarily in a degraded state, where messages may be lost in transmission. To counter such degraded paths, most of the service discovery protocols that we studied depend on a reliable transport service to send unicast messages and to receive replies. If unable to deliver a specific message within a bounded time, a reliable transport service will issue a remote exception. In such circumstances, an otherwise retrievable service description will not be obtained, unless a seeker retries the retrieval message persistently until successful.

5.1.2 Registration Guarantee. Service discovery systems that support repositories may allow services to deposit service descriptions on those repositories, which service seekers may query. In addition, some service discovery systems provide the option for service seekers to deposit standing queries (i.e., requests for notification) about changes in the state of service descriptions of interest. Similarly, some service discovery systems permit registration to receive events emitted to reflect changes in the state of selected variables. Registration is the act of depositing into a registry either: service descriptions, queries for service descriptions, or requests to receive variable events. We specify a *Registration* guarantee to define the circumstances under which such registration should succeed.

Assuming a registrant wishes to place a registration of a specified class (i.e., service descriptions, notification requests, or variable-event requests) into a registry, the registration can be considered to be *feasible* under the following conditions: (1) the registrant has discovered the registry, (2) the registry is capable of accepting registrations of the specified type, (3) the registration is not in the registry, and (4) the registrant and registry can communicate through a registration process active on an operational path. Given multiple (n) registrants that each wishes to place some number (r_n) of feasible registrations into the same registry, the total population of feasible registrations (p) for the registry is the sum of r_n over the n registrants. Assuming that the registry has the capacity to accept only m registrations, then eventually the number of registrations in the registry should be guaranteed to be the minimum of m or p. We call this the *Registration* guarantee, which is subject to the same qualifications as the *Indirect Discovery* guarantee.

5.1.3 Update Guarantees. From time to time, service descriptions (including repository descriptions) change; thus, service discovery systems must ensure that such changes are disseminated to all relevant parties. For this reason, we expect that, given a change in a service description, all seekers holding a previous copy of the service description will eventually achieve one of the following outcomes: (1) the updated service description replaces the earlier copy of the description or (2) the earlier copy of the description is purged. Our model requires each service description to include a service identifier and a sequence number. For a given service identifier, increasing sequence numbers indicate more recent copies of the associated service description. Assuming that a seeker holds a copy of a service description when another copy becomes available with the same service identifier and a larger sequence number, then the seeker should be guaranteed to eventually obtain the more recent copy (that has the larger sequence number) or to discard the outdated copy (that has the smaller sequence number). We call this the *Update* guarantee.

Most service discovery systems we examined include mechanisms that attempt to ensure satisfaction of this *Update* guarantee; however, procedures differ markedly with differences in the type of description being updated and in system architecture. For repository descriptions, a repository first locally updates the description; then, the advertiser is responsible for disseminating the update (as described in Section 3.2). For service descriptions, the service proxy updates the description locally, after which dissemination procedures differ with system architecture. In two-party architectures, the service proxy disseminates the update directly to seekers (as described in Section 3.4.4). In three-party architectures, the service proxy first propagates the update to relevant repositories, which then relay the change to seekers (as described in Section 3.4.2). Since the *Update* guarantee is subject to the same qualifications as the *Service Description Retrieval* guarantee, it is conceivable that a given seeker could fail to receive a specific update to a service description. In such situations, we would expect one of the discard guarantees (see Section 5.6 below) to apply; thus, the *Update* guarantee allows that one possible means to achieve consistency is simply to discard an outdated copy of a service description, relying on some later rediscovery action to acquire a current copy.

We have found that under certain circumstances some service discovery systems do not satisfy the *Update* guarantee. For example, when a seeker relies on a repository to issue notifications about an updated service description, temporary degradation of the communications path (between seeker and repository) can cause the notification to fail [18, 19]. Most service discovery protocols, which depend on a reliable transport service to deliver notifications, do not persist with attempts to deliver a notification after receiving an exception from the transport service. Instead, such systems seem to assume that subsequent attempts by a repository advertiser to deliver (discovery-related) lazy announcements (to the seeker) will also fail, leading the seeker to discard the repository description, and any related service descriptions. We have found circumstances where notifications fail due to temporary communications degradation, which does not impede a subsequent lazy announcement. In such circumstances, a seeker can continue to possess an outdated copy of a service description without being aware that a later copy exists. We have found instances of such behavior in both two-party and three-party architectures.

Before moving on to consider discard guarantees, we need to make some final points about the *Update* guarantee. As currently specified, the *Update* guarantee applies only to service descriptions (which include repository descriptions). The *Update* guarantee does not apply to administrative scopes because our model assumes these to be atomic names that may be added to or deleted from a set. Scope changes, then, can be detected under the terms of our *Discovery* guarantee (for scope additions) and our *Discovery Discard* guarantee (for scope deletions). Also, recall (Section 3.1) that our model allows service types to have attribute-based descriptions, much like service descriptions, which could lead to inconsistencies where a service description (which has a specified service type) is interpreted against an outdated service-type description. While our *Update* guarantee does not address this situation, we could define an additional guarantee that would look similar to the *Update* guarantee, except that the service description is replaced by a service-type description and a service-type identifier replaces the service identifier. Finally, a seeker could receive an updated service description that no longer satisfies its service requirements; in this case, the seeker should not accept the updated service description, but the outdated version should still be discarded from the seeker's cache.

5.1.4 Discard Guarantees. A secondary goal of service discovery systems is to detect and react to the loss of service availability, whether due to voluntary withdrawal or due to failures. In cases of service withdrawal, a service discovery system should seek to restore consistency by ensuring that all service seekers eventually learn that the withdrawn service is no longer available. In cases of failure, where a component is no longer accessible, affected parties should eventually detect such inaccessibility and discard information associated with the inaccessible component. We previously defined service guarantees related to acquisition of three types of information: discoverable items (including repository descriptions) found directly, without aid from a repository, service descriptions discovered indirectly, with aid from a repository, and registrations deposited on a registry. Below, we specify three service guarantees, each of which defines the circumstances under which an information holder should discard a related type of information, that is, a discoverable item, a service description obtained from a repository, or a registration deposited on a repository.

5.1.4.1 Discovery Discard. A seeker should discard information about a discoverable item upon learning that the item is no longer advertised or that the seeker can no longer communicate with the advertiser (for the item). We call this the *Discovery Discard* guarantee.

Due to various latencies inherent in a service discovery system, seekers may hold invalid information about a discoverable item during some period of inconsistency, whose duration depends upon the mechanism used to detect the inconsistency. Some service discovery systems include the capability for an advertiser to voluntarily withdraw a discoverable item (recall Section 3.2.4). Under voluntary withdrawal, inconsistency could last for the time it takes an advertiser to propagate the withdrawal message to a particular seeker. Of course, failure on a communication path between advertiser and seeker could result in failure to receive a withdrawal message–causing fallback to one of the remaining mechanisms: (1) soft-state or (2) application-level persistence. The soft-state mechanism requires that advertiser announcements for a discoverable item carry a time-to-live (TTL) that informs a seeker when to discard information associated with the item. The seeker then purges the information at the indicated time, unless another announcement arrives to extend the TTL. The soft-state mechanism ensures that the inconsistency will not extend beyond the TTL. Alternatively, using application-level persistence, a component could place an upper bound (UB) on the time during which it fails to communicate with a corresponding component. Information associated with the corresponding component would be discarded after reaching the UB. For example, a seeker who previously discovered a repository might reach the UB while attempting to query the repository for services or to renew registrations. The application-level persistence mechanism ensures any inconsistency will be remedied by the UB. When employing soft-state and application-level persistence in combination, any inconsistency should last for only the minimum of either the TTL or the UB.

Some of the service discovery systems we examined provide for voluntary withdrawal of discoverable items. All service discovery systems we examined support some form of the soft-state mechanism, and provide recommended TTL values that define the maximum period of inconsistency. When such systems are reconfigured (or deployed) with shorter or longer TTL values the periods of inconsistency will change accordingly. The application-level persistence mechanism is outside the scope of service discovery protocols; however, service discovery systems that use reliable transport services, which issue remote exceptions, can readily support the mechanism. When implementing application-level persistence the UB defines the period of inconsistency; however, the UB can be superceded when the service discovery system also includes a soft-state mechanism with TTL < UB. Finally, we note that the *Discovery Discard* guarantee applies only to SDEs; SDAs (service discovery applications) may take independent action with respect to the accessibility of the service provider. That is, since service providers and advertisers do not necessarily operate on the same node, it is conceivable that an advertiser could advertise a service description for a service provider that a discovering SDA cannot contact (see Section 3.6.4).

5.1.4.2 Description Discard. When service descriptions are discovered directly, without a repository, then the *Discovery Discard* guarantee applies; however, when service descriptions are discovered indirectly, from a repository, we must specify a separate guarantee to define the circumstances under which a service description should be discarded. Informally, this guarantee states that if a service seeker is holding a service description that is no longer maintained by a repository, or is maintained by a repository the seeker can no longer contact, then the seeker should eventually discard the service description. We call this the *Description Discard* guarantee.

Various latencies can lead to periods when the information held by service seekers is inconsistent with the information held by a repository. The duration of inconsistency depends upon the same factors described for the *Discovery Discard* guarantee. In our model, a service seeker may notify a supported SDA when a service description is discarded. The SDA may then take independent action to investigate the status of the service provider associated with the service description. That is, since service providers and repositories do not necessarily operate on the same node, it is conceivable that a service seeker could discard a service description for a service provider that a SDA can still contact (see Section 3.6.4).

5.1.4.3 Registration Discard. We define a *Registration Discard* guarantee: when a registrant and a registry cannot communicate about a registration, then the registration should be discarded eventually. A typical requirement for communication is that a registrant must periodically renew interest in a registration (recall Section 3.3); however, other forms of interaction might also be possible. For example, a registrant could choose to cancel a registration before a registry would otherwise discard it. Further, a registrant might update a registered service description (recall Section 3.4.2.1). Similarly, a registry might attempt to send notifications related to the registrations (recall Section 3.4.2.1 for service descriptions and Section 3.5 for variable events). The *Registration Discard* guarantee encompasses all forms of communication related to a particular registration, registrant, and registry. Of course, communication comes with a latency that could permit periods where registrant and registry hold an inconsistent view of a registration.

The duration of inconsistency depends upon the same factors as we discussed for the *Discovery Discard* guarantee, except that here the TTL is determined and granted by the registry (in cooperation with a related extension granter) when accepting a registration, and then updated by an extension granter with each request (from an extension requester) to renew the registration. The granted TTL competes with an upper bound (UB) that the registry might assign for other forms of interaction (e.g., attempting to send notifications or to grant extensions); thus, the inconsistency should last for the minimum of the TTL or the UB. For example, if a registrant registers with a registry to receive notification requests and subsequently the registry attempts unsuccessfully to issue a notification to the registrant, then the registry might have an UB for retrying failed notification attempts. If the UB is reached before the TTL, then the registry might choose to discard the related registration without waiting for an expected renewal. Of course, the registry might also choose to wait for the TTL to expire. Some service discovery systems we examined specify when to purge a registration, while other service discovery systems allow the flexibility for implementers to adopt their own policies. In addition, some service discovery systems specify different discard policies for different types of registrations.

5.2 Formalizing Service Guarantees. While an intuitive understanding of our proposed service guarantees can be quite informative, a more formal description is needed to encode the guarantees into a a form suitable for testing and measurement. Our UML model provides a suitable basis for such formalization. In what follows, we express our proposed service guarantees as consistency conditions, formalized in relationship to our UML model. The consistency conditions we define provide a means to concretely test operational systems to determine satisfaction of service guarantees. We have used these consistency conditions in several applications [17-21]. We expect that designers of service discovery protocols might be able to use these (or similar) consistency conditions to evaluate the correctness and performance of protocol designs.

We begin by describing our general notion of consistency condition. We then define the concept of *reachability* (used within several of our consistency conditions) in terms our UML model. Subsequently, we define consistency conditions related to discovery, registration, update, and discard guarantees.

5.2.1 Consistency Conditions. We express consistency conditions using first-order logic (FOL), extended with temporal logic [25]. We use FOL to express logical relationships between classes, attributes, operations and methods between our UML models. We occasionally employ standard mathematical functions to represent relations among quantities. We limit our use of temporal logic to the **EVENTUALLY** and **HENCEFORTH** operators, on which we place some qualifications.

We formulate consistency conditions along the following lines. Given a predicate P and some state S, $S[P]$ represents the value of P in state S. When $S[P]$ is true, P is said to hold in S. Given a predicate Q, a consistency condition is an implication of the form $P \rightarrow Q$, which means that when P holds, then Q must also hold for the condition to be satisfied. Satisfaction of a condition in state S occurs iff $S[P \& Q]$, indicating the system is consistent in state S. In contrast, when $S[P \& \sim Q]$, then the condition is not satisfied and the system is inconsistent in S. To define consistency conditions temporally, we use the **EVENTUALLY** operator to specify the value of a predicate at some future state of the system. Given predicates P and Q, the formula $P \rightarrow$ **EVENTUALLY** Q holds iff $S_i[P]$ and for some future state S_j, $S_j[Q]$, where $j > i$. During the operation of an actual system, satisfying the condition and reaching the consistent state S_j can be delayed by factors such as network failures, transmission delays, message losses, and algorithmic delays. During such delays, inconsistency persists temporarily prior to S_j.

The existence of delays implies that a predicate P could fail to hold long enough for predicate Q to be achieved, in which case the protocol cannot be expected to guarantee Q. However, if P continues to hold, the guarantee should be fulfilled eventually. To define the conditions under which success should be achieved, we use the temporal operator HENCEFORTH to specify that $S_j[P]$ holds for all future states, $j > i$. We express our consistency conditions in the form: **HENCEFORTH** $P \rightarrow$ **EVENTUALLY** Q. This formulation denotes the fact that if predicate P continues to hold, eventually Q will be achieved. In practical terms, this means that as long as P is true, a discovery system should strive to achieve Q; but once P no longer holds, then the system should not be expected to guarantee Q. Discovery protocols, when properly designed and deployed, should strive to ensure that: (1) the consistent state eventually becomes true and (2) the inconsistent state is bounded to as short an interval as possible. For a given service discovery protocol, if P does not hold long enough for Q to be achieved, then either: (1) a configuration error exists in a specific deployment, (2) user needs change at an unsupportable rate, or (3) the operating environment lacks sufficient stability (i.e., failures prevent the discovery protocol from achieving a consistent state). On the other hand, a design error likely exists if Q cannot be achieved even when P holds indefinitely.

5.2.2 Reachability . The concept of reachability is fundamental to our consistency conditions. Two SDEs are reachable for some specific function (e.g., discovery, service registration, or service retrieval) on some class of discoverable item (e.g., service description) if they are connected, and an appropriate process is active on the connection (i.e., the SDEs have implemented appropriate roles). Below, we define this concept more formally, in terms of the architectural framework depicted previously in Figure 2-5.

We say that two SDEs (service discovery entities), e_1 and e_2 (instances of some subclass of `ServiceDiscoveryEntity`) are connected if an operational communications path p (an instance of the class `Path`) exists between them, written $e_1.p.e_2$ in UML and p.up() is TRUE. Let t be an instance of the class `Process` running on path p, such that $p.t$.inProgress(). Let process t instantiate a service discovery function f that operates over some subclass $\bullet$ of discoverable items. To identify the instantiated service discovery function, we use the UML operation `isTypeOf`, which takes the name of the function as a parameter and returns a Boolean. We also extend the definition of `Process` given in Section 2.4 to add the attribute `Process.targetDiscoverableItem` to identify the subclass of `DiscoverableItem` operated on by the `Process`. Reachability between e_1 and e_2 for processes instantiating function f over discoverable items of class $\bullet$ is denoted with the predicate *Reachable* $(e_1, e_2, f, \bullet)$, which we define as

> **For all** e_1 and e_2 **if Henceforth**
> > **there exists** a p such that $(e_1.p.e_2$ **and** p.up()) **and**
> > **there exists** a t such that $p.t$.inProgress() **and**
> > **there exists** a f such that t.isTypeOf(f) **and**
> > **there exists** a $\bullet$ such that t.targetDiscoverableItem $= \bullet$
> **implies** *Reachable* $(e_1, e_2, f, \bullet)$

For example, *Reachable* $(e_1, e_2,$ Discovery, RepositoryDescription$)$ implies that SDEs e_1 and e_2 are reachable for purposes of discovering repository descriptions, as depicted in Figure 5-1.

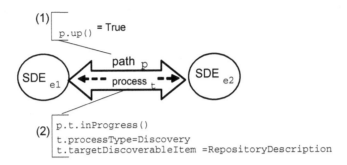

Figure 5-1. Example of Reachability for Discovery of Repository Descriptions

5.3 Discovery Consistency . We define two consistency conditions related to discovery. One condition formalizes the *Primary Discovery* guarantee and the other formalizes the *Secondary Discovery* guarantee.

5.3.1 Primary Discovery . Here, we specify conditions under which the seeker of some subclass of discoverable item should be able to obtain that item. Figure 5-2 provides the fragment of a related UML class diagram, which depicts two main types of SDEs: one (`SeekerEntity`) that assumes a seeker role and one (`AdvertiserEntity`) that assumes an advertiser role. For convenience, we define a `SeekerEntity`, which implements the class `Seeker` (specialized for a particular subclass of discoverable item) and a related `SeekerProxy`. Similarly, we define an `AdvertiserEntity`, which implements an `Advertiser` to publish a particular subclass of discoverable item. We define a *Primary Discovery consistency condition* over `SeekerEntity` and `AdvertiserEntity`.

Let m be the number of advertised discoverable items of class $\bullet$ available in some service discovery system. The *Primary Discovery* consistency condition sets forth the circumstances under which a seeker entity in need of n discoverable items of class $\bullet$ should eventually obtain the minimum of n and m. We first define the conditions for discovery of a single discoverable item.

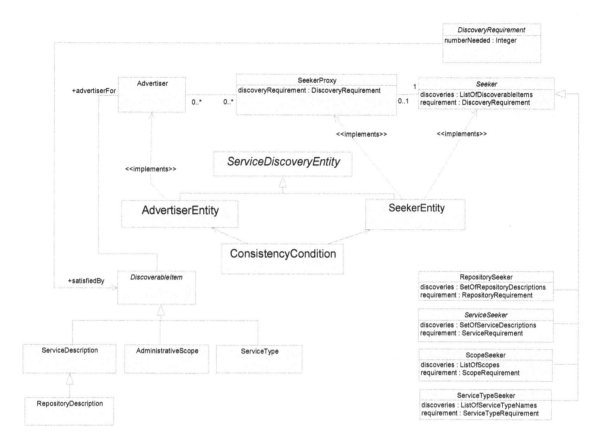

Figure 5-2. Context of Primary Discovery Consistency Condition

Let s be an instance of `SeekerEntity` that implements a subclass of `Seeker` specialized for discoverable items of class •. Let the discovery requirement for s be r (denoted by `s.requirement`). We define r to be an instance of a subclass of `DiscoveryRequirement` that is also specialized for a discoverable item of class • (see section 3.2 and Figure 3.2). Let a be an instance of an `AdvertiserEntity` for a discoverable item d of class • (represented by the association role name `advertiserFor` in figure 5.2), where r is satisfied by d (represented by the association role name `satisfiedBy`). Let s and a be reachable for discovery of items of class •, represented by the predicate *Reachable* (s, a, `Discovery`, •). The following expression defines the circumstances under which d is discoverable by seeker entity s and fulfills requirement r.

> **For all** s and a **if HENCEFORTH**
>   **there exists** a r such that `s.requirement` $= r$ **and**
>   **there exists** a d such that `d.advertiseFor= a` **and**
>   `d.isTypeOf(•)=` **TRUE and**
>   `r.satisfiedBy = d` **and**
>   *Reachable* (s, a, `Discovery`, •)
> **then** *Discoverable* (s, d, r)

That is, if a seeker with a requirement can reach the advertiser for a discoverable item d of class • and the discoverable item satisfies the requirement r, then the seeker should be able to obtain the discoverable item. This definition of discoverable is depicted in Figure 5-3.

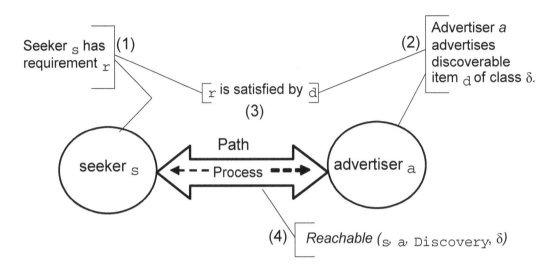

A seeker $_s$ should be able to discover a discoverable item $_d$ of type δ, if (1) $_s$ has a requirement $_r$ (2) if $_d$ is advertised by an advertiser $_a$, (3) $_r$ is satisfied by $_d$ and (4) $_s$ and $_a$ are reachable for discovery of items of type δ.

Figure 5-3. Illustrated Definition of Discoverable

Whether or not the seeker obtains the discoverable item is also contingent on the relationship between the number n of discoverable items that the seeker hopes to discover and the number m of suitable discoverable items available. Let $s.discoveries$ be the set of discoverable items currently held by $_s$. If $_d$ is an undiscovered discoverable item such that,

$$Discoverable\,(s,\,d,\,r) \wedge d \notin s.discoveries,$$

then the set D of undiscovered discoverable items for seeker $_s$ is given by

$$D = \{\,d\,\}\,Discoverable(s,d,r\ \wedge d \notin s.discoveries\ .$$

Let $m = |D|$, and define the predicate $NumberUndiscoveredDiscoverables\,(_s,\,_r,\,m)$, where m is the number of undiscovered discoverable items that satisfy a requirement $_r$ of seeker $_s$. Let $_s$ require n discoverable items that satisfy $_r$, given by $r.numberNeeded = n$. Then the *Primary Discovery* consistency condition states

For all s and r if **HENCEFORTH**
    there exists a m, such that *NumberUndiscoveredDiscoverables* (s, r, m) **and**
    there exists a n such that $r.\texttt{numberNeeded} = n$
then EVENTUALLY *NumberWillDiscover* $(s, r, \text{MIN}(m, n))$

where the predicate *NumberWillDiscover* specifies that seeker s discovers the minimum of n or m discoverable items that satisfy r. Given $m \geq n$, then eventually s should obtain n discoverable items. Given $m < n$, then the seeker should be expected to obtain only m discoverable items. This consistent state is illustrated in Figure 5-4.

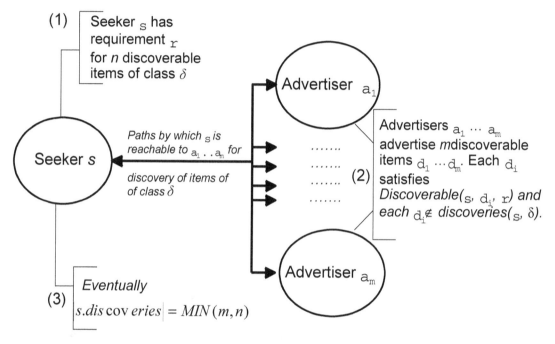

(1) Seeker s requires n discoverable items that satisfy requirement r, (2) there are m discoverable items that satisfy r that s has not discovered, then (3) *eventually* s discovers the minimum of m and n items.

Figure 5-4. Illustration of Consistent State for Primary Discovery

5.3.2 Secondary Discovery . Here, we specify conditions under which the seeker of a service description (for a non-repository service) should be able to discovery (or retrieve) a service description from a previously discovered repository. Figure 5-5 provides the fragment of a UML class diagram, which depicts two main types of SDEs: a `ServiceRetrievalEntity`, which assumes the unicast service-seeker role and implements the class `UnicastServiceSeeker`, and a `RepositoryEntity`, which assumes the service-repository role and implements the class `ServiceRepository`. We assume that the service retrieval entity has acquired access (through discovery processes) to the repository entity, and seeks to obtain service descriptions matching some requirement.

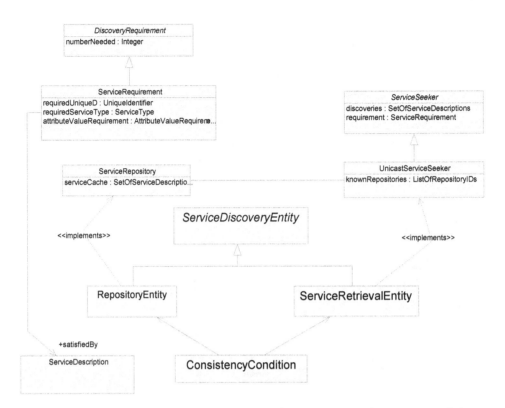

Figure 5-5. Context for Description Secondary Discovery Consistency Condition

Let s be an instance of `ServiceRetrievalEntity`, r be a an instance of `ServiceRequirement` that s seeks to satisfy, d be a service description and q be a an instance of `RepositoryEntity` with a service cache for service descriptions (shown in Figure 5.5 as `q.serviceCache`). Let s and q be reachable for purposes of retrieving service descriptions. We define the conditions under which a d that satisfies r will be retrievable by s from q. The UML associations `s.requirement` and `r.satisfiedBy` retain the same meaning as in the consistency condition for *Primary Discovery*.

> **For all** s, q, **and** d **if HENCEFORTH**
> **there exists** a r such that `s.requirement` $= r$ **and**
> *Reachable* (s, q, `Retrieval`, `ServiceDescription`) **and**
> $d \in$ `q.serviceCache` **and**
> `r.satisfiedBy` $= d$
> **then** *Retrievable* (s, d, r, q)

This definition of retrievable is illustrated in Figure 5-6 below.

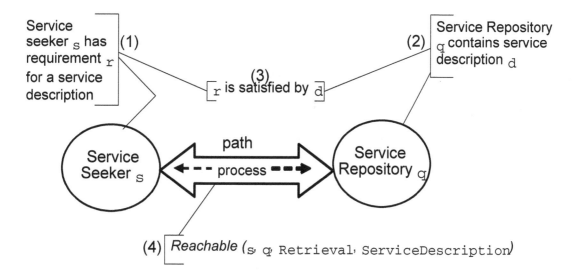

A seeker s should be able to retrieve a service description d from service repository q if (1) s has a requirement r (2) d is a member of the service cache of q, (3) r is satisfied by d, and (4) s and q are reachable for retrieval of service descriptions.

Figure 5-6. Illustrated Definition of Retrievable

Assume seeker s discovers a set of n repositories, each with a set S_i of service descriptions such that

$$S_i = \{ d \} Retrievable(s, d, r, q \wedge d \notin s.\texttt{discoveries} .$$

The available number of service descriptions that s can retrieve is given by

$$m_{Total} = \sum_{i=1}^{n} |Si| .$$

Let s require n service descriptions that satisfy r, given by $r.\texttt{numberNeeded} = n$, and the predicate *NumberUnretrieved*(s, r, ServiceDescription, m_{Total}) denote that seeker s with requirement r can retrieve at most m_{Total} service descriptions. The number of service descriptions that s should eventually discover is defined by the following consistency condition.

> **For all s and r if HENCEFORTH**
> **there exists a m such that** *NumberUnretrieved*(s, r, ServiceDescription, m_{Total})
> **there exists a n such that** $r.\texttt{numberNeeded} = n$
> **then EVENTUALLY** *NumberRetrieved* (s, ServiceDescription, MIN(n, m_{Total}))

This consistent state is illustrated in Figure 5-7 below.

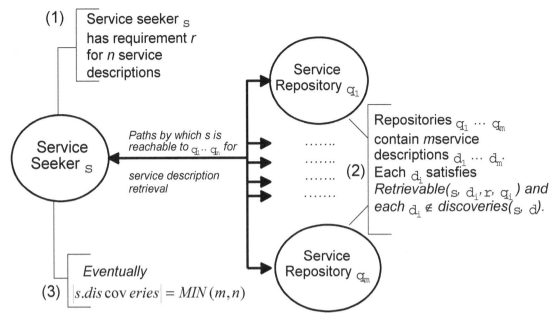

(1) Service seeker $_s$ has requirement r for n service descriptions

Service Seeker $_s$

Paths by which s is reachable to $q_1 .. q_m$ for

service description retrieval

Service Repository q_1

Service Repository q_m

Repositories $q_1 \cdots q_m$ contain m service descriptions $d_1 \cdots d_m$. (2) Each d_i satisfies *Retrievable($_s$, d_i, r, q_i) and each $d_i \notin$ discoveries($_s$, d).*

(3) $|s.\mathrm{dis\,cov\,}eries| = MIN\,(m,n)$

Eventually

(1) Seeker $_s$ requires n service descriptions, (2) there are m retrievable service descriptions that $_s$ has not retrieved, then (3) *eventually* $_s$ retrieves the minimum of m and n items.

Figure 5-7. Illustration of Consistent State for Secondary Discovery

5.4 Registration Consistency . Here, we specify the circumstances under which a registrant should successfully deposit a registration on a registry. Figure 5-8 contains the fragment of a related UML class diagram, which depicts two main types of SDEs: one `RegistrationSeekerEntity` that assumes a registration-requester role and implements the `RegistrationRequester` class and one `RegistryEntity` that implements the registry role and implements the `Registry` class. As described in Section 3.3.2, the `RegistrationRequester` may be specialized as any of the following subclasses: `ServiceRegistrationRequester`, `Notification RegistrationRequester` and `EventRegistrationRequester`, depending upon the type of information to be deposited on the registry. Similarly, `Registry` may be specialized as a `ServiceRegistry`, `NotificationRequestRegistry`, `FullRegistry`, or `VariableEvenRegistry` according to the type of information that it will accept. We assume that the registry has been previously discovered (via discovery of the associated repository) and made available to the registration seeker entity.

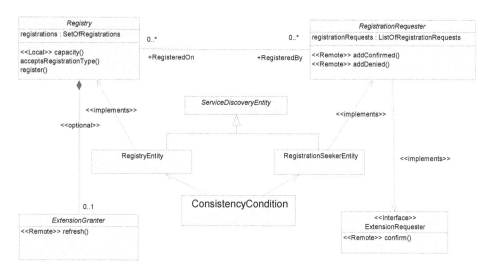

Figure 5-8. Context for Registration Consistency Condition

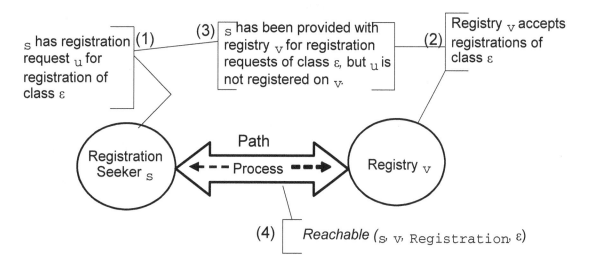

A registration seeker $_s$ should be able to register $_u$ with registry $_v$ if (1) $_u$ is a registration request for registrations of class ε (2) $_v$ accepts registrations of class ε, (3) $_s$ has been provided with $_v$ as a registry for registrations of class ε, but $_s$ has not yet registered $_u$ on $_v$ and (4) $_s$ and $_v$ are reachable to register registrations of class ε.

Figure 5-9. Illustrated Definition of Registerable

Let $_s$ be an instance of a RegistrationSeekerEntity and $_v$ be an instance of a RegistryEntity. Let $_u$ be an instance of a RegistrationRequest for registrations of subclass $\bullet$ (either ServiceRegistration, Notification Registration, or ServiceVariableRegistration), where $_s$ holds $_u$ (e.g., $_u$ $\in$ s.registrationRequests, and let $_v$ be a registry that accepts registrations of class $\bullet$ (as indicated by the operation v.acceptsRegistrationType ($\bullet$)). We assume v has been provided to s for purposes of registration (represented by $v \in$ s·knownRegistries. We also assume that s and v are reachable for registration of requests of class •, and u is not yet registered with v. The circumstances under which s can attempt to register u with v is formalized as

For all s and v if HENCEFORTH
  there exists a u such that $u \in$ s·registrationRequests **and**
  u·registrationType $= \bullet$ **and**
  v·acceptsRegistrations(•) **and**
  $v \in$ s·knownRegistries **and**
  $u \notin$ s·registrations **and**
  Reachable (s, v, Registration, •)
then *Registerable* (s, v, u)

Informally, if a registration seeker entity s has been given a registration request u (of class •) and a registry entity v that can accept registration requests (of class •) and if s and v are reachable for purposes of registration of requests of class • and if u is not yet registered on v, then s should be able to register u on v. We illustrate this definition of a registerable registration in Figure 5-9. Of course, we must consider the fact that a registry entity has a finite capacity to accept registrations.

Let S be the set of all registration seeker entities s for which v is a known registry

$$S = \{s\} \colon v \in s.\text{knownRegistries} .$$

Let z be the number of registration requests held by s, or $z = |s.registrationRequests|$.

We compute the number of (*Registrable*) registration requests n_T pending for v as

$$n_T = \sum_{S} \sum_{i=1}^{z} x_i$$

where

$$x_i = \begin{cases} 1 & \text{if } Registerable(s, v, u_i) \\ 0 & \text{otherwise} \end{cases}.$$

The predicate *TotalNumberRegisterable*(v, n_T) holds when n_T registrations are pending for registry v across all registration seeker entities in S. Recall in section 3.3 we introduced the operation v·capacity() to denote that registry v has capacity to accept m additional registrations. Accordingly, we should expect that

For all v if HENCEFORTH
  there exists a n_T such that *TotalNumberRegisterable* (v, n_T) **and**
  there exists a m such that v·capacity $= m$
then EVENTUALLY *NumberRegistered* (v, MIN(n_T, m))

where the predicate *NumberRegistered*(v, x) denotes that registry v contains x registrations. Informally, given n_T qualified registrations for registry v, which has capacity to accept m additional registrations, then eventually the minimum of n_T or m registrations should be deposited with v. This consistent state illustrated in Figure 5-10.

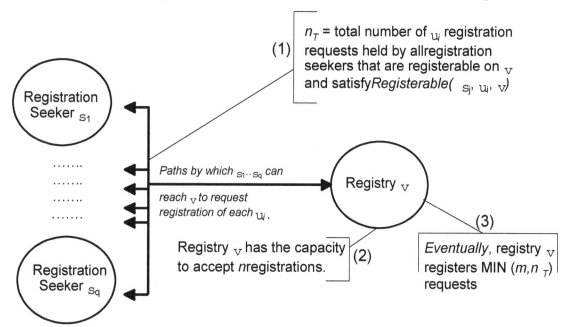

(1) The total number of registration requests of all registration seekers that are registerable on registry v is n_T, (2) the capacity of registry v is m, then (3) *eventually* the number of requests that are registered on v is the minimum of m and n_T.

Figure 5-10. Illustration of Consistent State for Registration

5.5 Update Consistency. Here, we specify the circumstances under which a component should either: (1) replace outdated information with updated information or (2) discard the outdated information. Let s be an instance of `ServiceSeeker` and d be an instance of `ServiceDescription`, where the updated successor of d is denoted as d' and has an incremented sequence number. We illustrate this consistent state in Figure 5-11.

For all s **if**
    there exists a d such that $d \in$ `s.discoveries` **and**
    HENCEFORTH **there exists** a d' **such that**
        (d'.serviceID = d.serviceID **and**
         d'.sequenceNumber > d.sequenceNumber)
  then EVENTUALLY
    (d' $\in$ s.discoveries) **and**
    d $\notin$ s.discoveries)
      or
    (d' $\notin$ s.discoveries) **and**
    d $\notin$ s.discoveries))

We illustrate this consistent state in Figure 5-11.

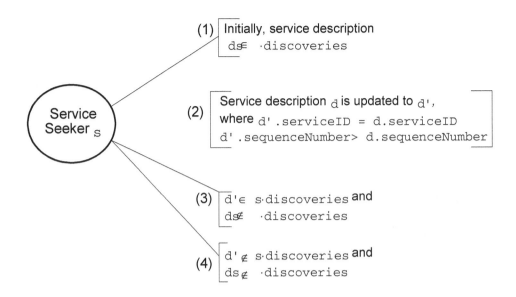

(1) A service seeker s has discovered a service description d, (2) d is updated to d', then either(3) d' replaces d on s, (i.e. $d' \in s \cdot discoveries$ and d is purged by s such that $d \notin s.discoveries$, or (4) in the update to d' never arrives and eventually d is purged by s.

Figure 5-11. Illustration of Consistent State for Update

5.6 Discard Consistency. In what follows, we define a consistency condition to formalize each discard guarantee: the *Discovery Discard* guarantee, the *Description Discard* guarantee, and the *Registration Discard* guarantee.

5.6.1 Discovery Discard. Here, we specify the circumstances under which a seeker of discoverable items should discard previously discovered information. Informally, a seeker should discard information about a discoverable item when the item is no longer advertised or when a seeker and advertiser (for the item) can no longer communicate.

Let s be an instance of SeekerEntity, a be an instance of AdvertiserEntity, and d be an instance of a discoverable item of class $\bullet$, as defined in section 5.5.3.1. Discoverable item d should be discarded by s under the following conditions.

> **For all s and a if**
>   **there exists a d such that $d \in s \cdot discoveries$ and**
> $d \cdot isTypeOf(\bullet)$ **and**
>   **HENCEFORTH**
>   **((there does not exist an a such that $d \cdot advertiserFor = a$ or**
>   **(there exists an a such that $d \cdot advertiserFor = a$ and**
>   **not *Reachable* $(s, a, Discovery, \bullet)))$**
>   **then EVENTUALLY $d \notin s \cdot discoveries$**

We illustrate this consistent state in Figure 5-12.

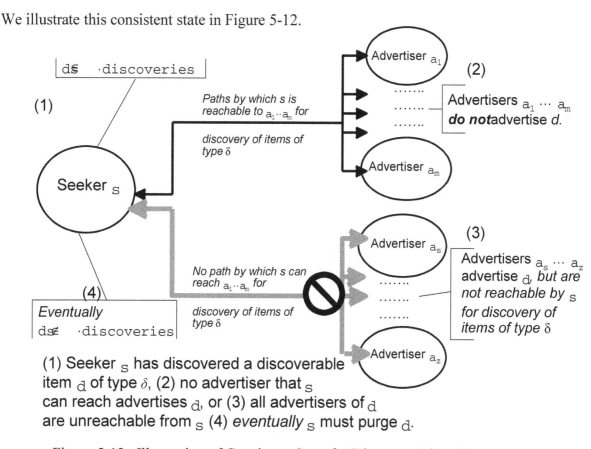

(1) Seeker $_s$ has discovered a discoverable item $_d$ of type δ, (2) no advertiser that $_s$ can reach advertises $_d$, or (3) all advertisers of $_d$ are unreachable from $_s$ (4) *eventually* $_s$ must purge $_d$.

Figure 5-12. Illustration of Consistent State for Discovery Discard

5.6.2 Description Discard. When service descriptions are discovered without a repository, then the *Discovery Discard* condition applies; however, when service descriptions are discovered from a repository, we must specify a separate *Description Discard* condition to define circumstances under which a service description should be discarded. Informally, if a seeker is holding a service description that is no longer maintained by a repository, or is maintained by a repository the seeker can no longer contact, then the seeker should eventually discard the service description. We specify the *Description Discard* condition more formally below.

Let $_s$ be an instance of `UnicastServiceSeeker`, $_q$ be an instance of `RepositoryEntity`, and $_d$ be an instance of `ServiceDescription` as defined in section 5.5.3.2.

> **For all** $_s$ and $_q$ **if**
>   **there exists** a $_d$ **such that** $d \in$ s.discoveries **and**
>   **HENCEFORTH**
>   ($d \notin$ q.serviceCache **or**
>   ($d \in$ q.serviceCache **and**
>   **not** *Reachable* (s, q, Retrieval, ^{S}erviceDescription))
>   **then EVENTUALLY** $d \notin$ s.discoveries

We illustrate this consistent state below in Figure 5-13.

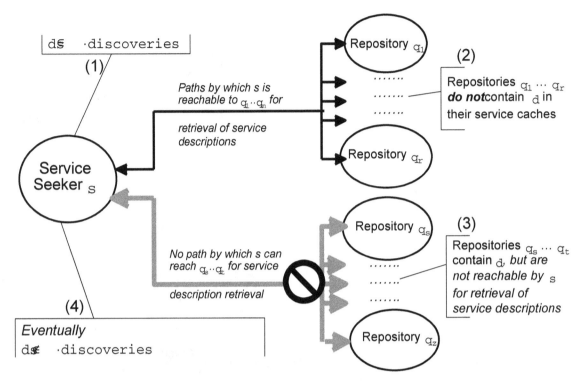

$ds = \cdot$discoveries (1)

Paths by which s is
reachable to $q_1 \cdots q_n$ for

retrieval of service
descriptions

Service
Seeker s

(2)

Repositories $q_1 \cdots q_r$
do notcontain d in
their service caches

No path by which s can
reach $q_s \cdots q_t$ for service

description retrieval

(4)

(3)

Repositories $q_s \cdots q_t$
contain d, *but are*
not reachable by s
for retrieval of
service descriptions

Eventually
$ds \neq \cdot$discoveries

(1) Seeker s has a service description, (2) any repository that s can
reach does not cache d, (3)no repository that caches d can be
reached from s, (4) *eventually* s must purge d.

Figure 5-13. Illustration of Consistent State for Description Discard

5.6.3 Registration Discard. Here, we specify the circumstances under which a registry
should discard information about a registration. Informally, if a registrant and a registry
cannot communicate about a registration, then the registration should be discarded
eventually.

Let s be an instance of `RegistrationSeekerEntity`, v be an instance of
`RegistryEntity`, and u be an instance of a `Registration` as defined in section
5.4. Further, let $\cdot$ be a class of registration requests and g some registration-related
function, constrained as follows. If $\cdot$ is a `ServiceRegistration`, then g must be
either: a registration extension, cancellation, or service change. If $\cdot$ is a
`NotificationRegistration`, then g must be either: a registration extension,
cancellation, or notification. If $\cdot$ is a `ServiceVariableRegistration`, then g
must be either: a registration extension, cancellation, or event notification.

For all s and v **if**
    there exists a u such that $u \in v \cdot$registrations **and**
    u.isTypeOf($\cdot$) **and**
    HENCEFORTH not *Reachable* ($s, v, g, \cdot$))
then EVENTUALLY $u \notin v \cdot$registrations

We illustrate this consistent state in Figure 5-14 below.

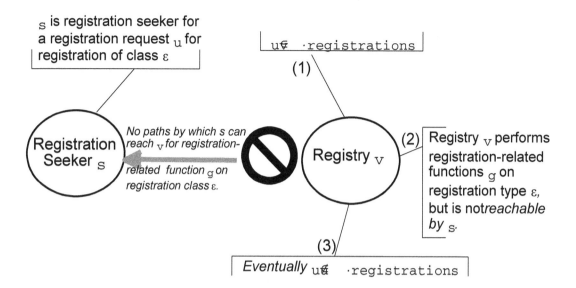

(1) Registration seeker $_s$ has previously registered registration request $_u$ of type ε on registry $_v$, (2) $_v$ is no longer reachable by $_s$ to perform registration functions $_g$ related to registration class ε (3) *eventually* $_v$ must purge $_u$.

Figure 5-14. Illustration of Consistent State for Registration Discard

6. Representing Specific Service Discovery Systems

As presented to this point our model of service discovery systems is abstract and generic, that is, we have not represented any specific service discovery systems. In this section, we illustrate how our model can be used to represent some concrete service discovery systems. For example, we map UPnP [5] (Section 6.1), Jini [1] (Section 6.2), and SLP [3] (Section 6.3) to our model. We use our model to represent Web Services Dynamic Discovery [9] (Section 6.3) and the Globus Monitoring and Discovery Service [10] (Section 6.4), two discovery systems that were not part of the group we studied as we developed our generic model.

6.1 UPnP. UPnP embodies a two-party architecture of control points (clients) and root devices (service proxies). UPnP root devices can contain and advertise a hierarchy of embedded devices and services. The complex nested structure allows UPnP root devices to function as a repository for a set of devices or services. To advertise repository contents, root devices send periodic multicast announcements for the root device itself, and for each embedded device contained within the root device. Root devices also announce the types of embedded devices and services. UPnP control points may listen for announcements, and respond with requests for more detailed information about a device or service of interest. Control points may also issue multicast queries for specific devices (root or embedded), services, and service types. Root devices listen for such queries and respond as appropriate. UPnP also allows control points to subscribe for notification of changes in the state of variables maintained by services of interest.

6.1.1 UPnP Discovery. UPnP supports discovery of three kinds of discoverable items: repository descriptions for root devices, service descriptions for embedded devices, and service type descriptions. In terms of our model (see Figure 6-1), UPnP root devices (represented as a `SeekerProxySDE`) implement the advertiser role (`Advertiser`) for these items, while control points (represented as a `ClientSDE`) implement the seeker roles (`RepositorySeeker` and `SeekerProxy`). All root devices also implement the repository role, but limited to the type `ServiceRepository`, since UPnP root devices do not support service registration or notification-request registration. UPnP does not directly support administrative scopes, though root devices may be used to achieve *de facto* scope partitioning. Root devices may advertise, and control points may seek, embedded devices and service types. Embedded devices have their own service descriptions; service types have service-attribute descriptions (omitted from Figure 6-1).

UPnP supports both lazy and aggressive discovery. In lazy discovery, advertisers broadcast sets of announcements in cycles separated by a minimum of 1800 s. The announcement cycles continue for the lifetime of the root device. Within each cycle, advertisers may interleave announcements for the root-device repository with announcements for embedded devices and service types contained within the repository. UPnP requires that announcements be replicated (separated by a short interval) as follows: three announcements for the root-device repository, followed by two announcements for each embedded device and its device types, and one announcement for each contained service type. Each announcement consists of a partial description of the related root device, embedded device or service type. Upon receipt, the control point first caches the root-device repository address on its "discoveries" list. The client must then initiate a series of HTTP-GET requests using the reliable TCP protocol to obtain the entire list of service descriptions for the root device, the embedded devices and associated services, and the service types. The HTTP-GET operation does not permit selective retrieval; instead the service descriptions for all items within the root device are transmitted as a formatted text stream, a potential disadvantage if this content is large. The control point must provide the logic to parse the description and locate needed services.

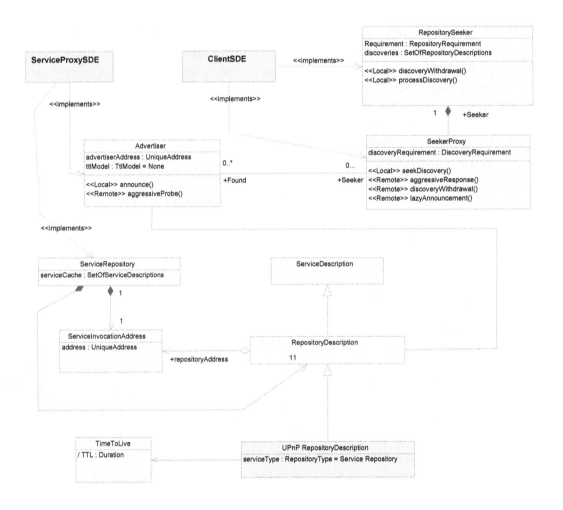

Figure 6-1. Class Diagram for UPnP Repository Discovery

Control points hold discoveries for a TTL that is tied to the announcement cycle; hence UPnP is modeled with the *correlated* type of TTL-computation algorithm. The advertiser must issue subsequent announcements prior to the TTL to refresh the discovery; otherwise, the control point may purge the discovery from its "discoveries" list. The advertiser also may issue a `discoveryWithdrawal()` for a root-device repository and its contents at the end of a scheduled lifetime, or before, if necessary.

While lazy discovery proceeds for the lifetime of a root-device repository, the control point may launch aggressive discovery queries on demand, using the local operation `seekDiscovery()` in the `SeekerProxy`. The UPnP `aggressiveProbe()` permits specification of selection criteria, allowing the seeker to search for specific root-device repositories, embedded devices, and service types. The probe is multicast using the model of periodicity for aggressive discovery described in Section 3.2.2. If the selection criteria match, an advertiser replies directly (i.e., unicast) to the seeker with an appropriate subset of the same messages used in lazy announcements. The seeker then issues HTTP-GET requests to obtain a complete description of the contents held by the root-device repository.

6.1.2 Service Description Monitoring Through Variable Monitoring. UPnP supports service-variable monitoring procedures that closely resemble the capabilities described in Section 3.5, and hence need not be restated here. The variable-query capability supports polling of service variables that are made available by a service provider for this purpose. UPnP also permits registration for events that indicate changes to service variables on the same basis. Though UPnP does not provide specific mechanisms for monitoring service descriptions, a root device could designate a service variable to indicate when a service description changes and could make the designated variable available to control points, either for polling or notification or both. Upon learning of a change, the control point must send an HTTP-GET to obtain the full service description, and then find the change by comparing the new service description with a previously cached copy.

6.2 Jini. Jini supports a three-party architecture, where services and clients both seek to discover lookup services (i.e., repositories). Jini services register service descriptions on discovered repositories, while Jini clients retrieve service descriptions from discovered repositories. Clients may submit unicast `findService()` queries to look for services and may register for notification about changes in services of interest. Jini allows clients and services to locate repositories (and also allows repositories to discover each other) using lazy, aggressive, and directed discovery. While Jini supports administrative scopes, it provides no inherent mechanisms to discover scopes, service types, and service-attributes types. For this reason, Jini components (clients, services, and repositories) must be configured with information about available scopes and service types.

6.2.1 Jini Discovery. A Jini lookup service implements the repository and advertiser roles, while clients and services implement repository-seeker roles. This is represented in Figure 6-2 by the `ServiceRepository` and `Advertiser` classes for the lookup service (`DirectorySDE`) and by the `RepositorySeeker` and `SeekerProxy`[1] for client (`ClientSDE`) and service (`ServiceProxySDE`). The lookup service also has an associated `RepositoryDescription` that includes a list of configured administrative scopes. Jini lookup services are specialized as full registries that provide for registration of service descriptions and notification requests (as described below in Section 6.2.2).

---

[1] To allow lookup services to discover each other, they also implement the `RepositorySeeker` and `SeekerProxy` classes, which we omit from Figure 6-2 to simplify the figure.

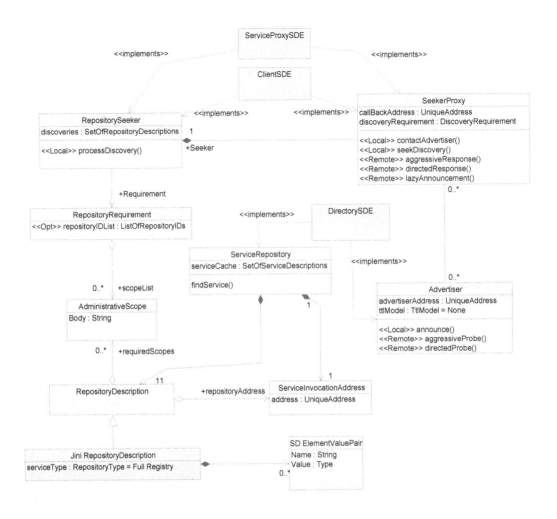

Figure 6-2. Class Diagram for Jini Repository Discovery

Jini lazy-discovery procedures require repository advertisers to multicast an announcement message, `lazyAnnouncement()`, periodically at a recommended interval of 120 s. These announcements continue for the life of the repository. Each announcement contains only the advertiser's callback address and the list of scopes configured for the repository. Seekers, acting for clients or service proxies, maintain a `RepositoryRequirement` with a list of required scopes in which they seek repositories. Upon receipt of an announcement, a seeker in need of additional repositories checks for intersection between the scope list in its `RepositoryRequirement` and the scope list in the announcement. If the scope lists intersect, the seeker initiates a unicast TCP connection to the advertiser to obtain the related repository description, which includes an address for interacting with the repository. In contrast to UPnP, Jini does not support a repository TTL; however the repository seeker may use subsequent lazy announcements as a heartbeat mechanism.

Jini aggressive discovery procedures, launched when a seeker (client or service proxy) invokes `seekDiscovery()` to send `aggressiveProbe()` messages to any reachable advertisers, are initiated upon component startup and may subsequently be invoked on demand. As a recommended default, a Jini aggressive-discovery sequence consists of seven multicast probes spaced five seconds apart. The initial aggressive-probe sequence allows a repository seeker to locate available repositories in its locale. Each probe contains the seeker callback address, a list of target administrative scopes, and a "previous responders list" to allow advertisers to suppress duplicate responses. If an advertiser receives a probe from a seeker to which it has not previously responded and the seeker's scope requirements intersect with the advertiser's configured scopes, then the advertiser initiates a unicast TCP connection to the seeker callback address to convey the advertiser's network address. The seeker can then obtain a copy of the associated repository description.

Jini also provides a directed-discovery process in which the repository seeker invokes a local method, `contactAdvertiser()`, to stimulate a TCP connection to each member of a list of network addresses for advertisers. A contacted advertiser uses the connection to provide its related repository description to the seeker. Once a repository description is cached, a seeker can listen for lazy announcements to ensure the repository remains advertised (and therefore available). Jini does not support discovery withdrawal.

After discovering a repository, a Jini client may search (by sending unicast `findService()` messages) within the repository for service descriptions of interest, or may register to be notified of updates regarding service descriptions of interest. Unlike in UPnP, Jini queries may specify matching criteria consisting of ServiceIDs for specific services that are needed, or combinations of desired service types and service description attribute values. Jini repositories return a set of `ServiceDescriptions` matching the query. Jini service descriptions include all information needed to access the service provider immediately, including a description of the service API, and a service invocation address, and, optionally, an address to retrieve any associated GUI. Unlike UPnP, the Jini service description has no TTL; therefore, the client must monitor the status of the service description through other means (see Section 6.2.2 below).

Jini allows   repository seekers to dynamically add and delete scopes to the `RepositoryRequirement`. This action may trigger the seeker to search for new repositories. Deleting a scope will cause the affected repository seeker to purge any cached discoveries whose scope list no longer intersects the required scope list. This action then stimulates deregistration of any service or notification-request registrations made on the registry for the related repository. While the core Jini specification does not support dynamic scope change for repositories, the Jini code includes an administrative API that provides a method for this purpose. Jini provides no direct means to notify repository seekers of such a scope change. To learn of scope changes, seekers listen for subsequent lazy announcements.

6.2.2 Service and Notification Request Registration. Jini repositories implement the role of full registries, permitting registration of service descriptions by service proxies and registration of notification requests by clients. In our model, Jini service proxies implement the class `ServiceRegistrationRequester`, while clients implement the class `NotificationRegistrationRequester`. Jini implements registration and extension procedures that closely follow Section 3.3. In registration extension, Jini registries assume the role of extension granters using the additive strategy, while clients and service proxies assume the role of extension requesters. Jini service proxies are required to register all service descriptions they manage with each repository they discover. The registration of notification requests by clients is discretionary. A client may register to receive notices of "Arrival", "Departure", and "Change" events concerning service descriptions that meet criteria specified in the `NotificationScope` that accompanies each registration request. Jini `NotificationRequests` contain `NotficationTypes` and `NotificationScopes` that closely match descriptions in Section 3.3, but exclude an administrative scope list. In Jini, if a repository seeker purges a repository discovery, the related registration requester (for a service or notification request) must deregister previous registrations from the registry for the repository.

6.2.3 Service Description Monitoring. Jini clients monitor repositories for changes to service descriptions. To update a service description, a Jini service proxy first sends the updated information to all repostiories on which the description is registered by means of unicast `changeServiceDescription()` messages, described in Section 3.4. If a client has registered to receive a "Change" notification type for the related service description, the repository issues a notification to the client. Otherwise the client must be configured to poll, using `findService()`, repositories for updates to service descriptions of interest. Jini does not define any direct communication between client and service proxy, though service providers that use Jini may support service variable monitoring (described in Section 3.5). Since Jini service descriptions have no TTL, clients can learn of service unavailability through one of three methods: (1) by registering for "Departure" notifications, (2) by queries that indicate that the service description is no longer cached by the repository, or (3) by unsuccessful attempts to invoke the service.

6.3 SLP. Like Jini, SLP supports a three-party architecture; however, SLP can operate in a two-party mode when no repositories are available. In the three-party architecture, SLP Service Agents (service proxies) discover and register service descriptions on Directory Agents (repositories) and User Agents (clients) discover repositories to query for service descriptions. SLP does not allow clients to register requests for notification of changes in services of interest. In the SLP two-party mode, clients discover and query service proxies. SLP enables discovery of repository descriptions in either three-party (where repositories represent Directory Agents) or two-party (where repositories represent Service Agents) operation. The SLP two-party mode also allows discovery of individual service descriptions, as well as configuration information (such as available scopes, service types, and service-attribute types). SLP supports lazy, aggressive, and directed discovery in either the three-party architecture or the two-party mode.

6.3.1 SLP Discovery. To discover repositories in the three-party architecture, both service proxies and clients implement the repository seeker role, through the `RepositorySeeker` and `SeekerProxy` classes, while repositories implement the repository and advertiser roles, through the `ServiceRepository` and `Advertiser` classes, respectively. Advertisers operate on behalf of `RepositoryDescriptions`. In two-party mode, service proxies implement the advertiser role through the

`Advertiser` class, and may also implement the repository role if they manage one or more service descriptions. Correspondingly, clients implement the role of repository seekers in the three-party architecture case but become service seekers in the two-party mode. Our model of the SLP three-party architecture is shown in Figure 6-3, while Figure 6-4 depicts a two-party configuration (including some service-agent repositories).

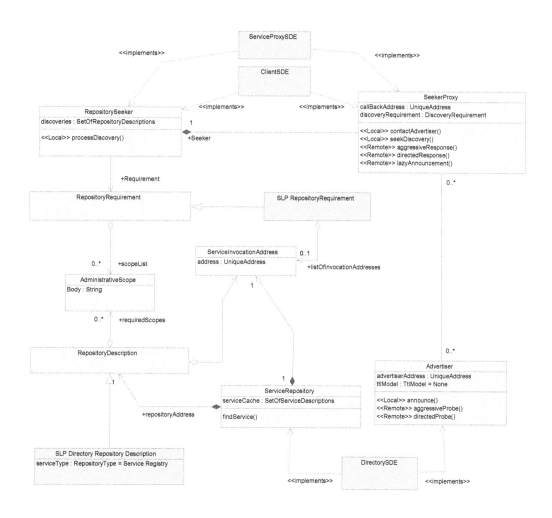

Figure 6-3 Class Diagram for SLP Discovery in Three-Party Mode

A SLP service discovery system may be configured to operate exclusively as either a three- or two-party architecture. SLP may also be configured as a three-party system in which clients switch to two-party mode when no directory agents are available. Upon failure to locate at least one directory agent, a client launches an aggressive-discovery sequence to search for service proxies, and begins listening for lazy announcements from service proxies. The client caches any discovered service proxies and related service descriptions, but also continues to search for directory agents. Upon eventually finding a directory agent, the client discards service-proxy discoveries, but retains previously cached service descriptions. Subsequently, the client interacts with the directory agent, as long as it remains available.

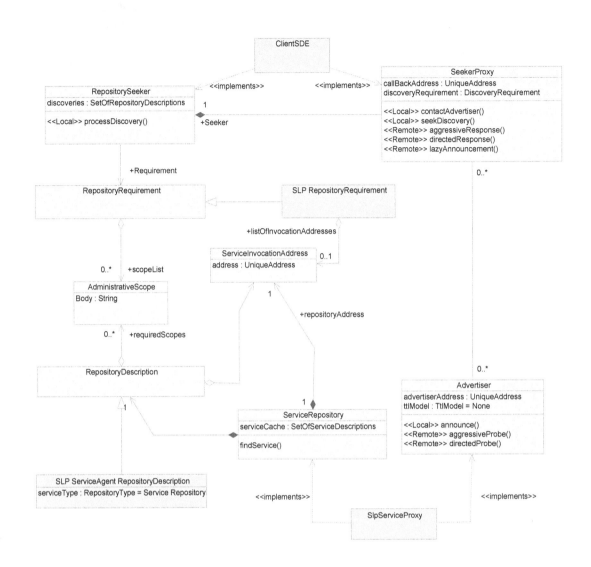

Figure 6-4 Class Diagram for SLP Discovery in Two-Party Mode

Like Jini, SLP supports repository descriptions that consist of a Repository ID and a scope list. SLP directory-agent repositories are of the type "Service Registry", while (two-party) service-agent repositories are of the type "Service Repository". Service proxies and clients maintain a `RepositoryRequirement` that specifies desired Repository IDs or a list of required administrative scopes. SLP designates a default scope that encompasses all service discovery entities (where partitioning by scope is undesired). Otherwise, SLP repositories are configured at start-up time with a list of scopes that must be matched to the scope lists of repository requirements maintained by repository seekers. In the three-party architecture, service proxies and clients seek directory agents with intersecting scope lists; in two-party mode, clients seek service agents on the same basis. Repository descriptions cached by the Seeker consist solely of the repositories' network address.

SLP supports lazy and aggressive repository discovery, as well as directed discovery in the three-party architecture and the two-party mode. In SLP lazy discovery, advertisers multicast individual announcements periodically at recommended intervals of 10,800 s. Each announcement contains a list of scopes configured for the repository and a callback address. In the three-party architecture, a seeker (for a service proxy or client) listens for announcements when in need of directory agents. If the scope list in an announcement intersects the scope list in a seeker's repository requirement, then the seeker caches the repository description. Each service-agent seeker will immediately register its service descriptions with each discovered directory agent. User-agent seekers may initiate a `findService()` query to a discovered directory agent in order to search for service descriptions. In the two-party mode, a client that locates a service-agent repository with an intersecting scope list caches the address through which to query the repository. Like Jini, SLP does not limit repository lifetime; hence, repository discoveries are retained until `findService()` attempts fail or according to some other application-level policy. SLP does not support repository withdrawal.

In aggressive discovery, seekers call the local `seekDiscovery()` operation to initiate a sequence of `aggressiveProbe()` messages, which consist of six multicast probes over a 15-s period. In the three-party architecture, this sequence is executed when a repository seeker first starts up, and is repeated thereafter every 900 s, or as needed to discover directory agents. SLP also allows seekers to discover administrative scopes, service types, and service-attribute types by sending aggressive probes; directory agents and service agents may implement advertisers that listen for, and reply to, such probes. As in Jini, each SLP probe contains the list of scopes configured for the seeker and a list of previous responders. A receiving repository, whose scope list intersects with the scope list in the probe, will respond if not among the previous responders. Upon receiving the response, a seeker may cache the discovery and initiate appropriate interactions. SLP supports directed discovery by allowing a repository seeker to obtain (by some external mechanism) addresses for repository advertisers that should respond if available. Unlike Jini, SLP does not permit scopes to be added or deleted during operation; and no mechanisms are provided for dynamic scope change. In two-party mode, clients execute the aggressive-discovery sequence when attempting to discover service agents.

Like Jini, SLP supports a unicast `findService()`, directed by clients to directory agents in the three-party architecture and to service agents in two-party mode. Queries may be sent as needed after repository discovery. Also like Jini and unlike UPnP, queries may specify matching criteria consisting of desired ServiceIDs or combinations of service types and descriptive service-attribute values. SLP repositories return a set of addresses for services that match the query. The client must then use these addresses to obtain the full service description, including the location of the service provider; the details of this process are not defined in the SLP specification.

6.3.2 Service Registration. SLP directory agents implement the service registry role, as described in Section 3.3, permitting registration of service descriptions by service proxies who, according to our model, would implement the service registration requester role through the `ServiceRegistrationRequester` class. Service registrations can be extended based on the assignment strategy, using procedures described in 3.3 with directory agents assuming the extension-granter role and service agents assuming the extension-requester role. As in Jini, SLP service agents are required to register all of their service descriptions on each directory agent that they discover and cache. SLP does not support registration of notification requests by clients.

6.3.3 Service Description Monitoring. In the three-party architecture, clients monitor changes to service descriptions through directory agents. To update a service description that it previously registered with a directory agent, a service agent invokes the `changeServiceDescription()` operation. In SLP, this effectively reregisters the service description by overwriting the previous registration and assigning a new TTL. A client must be configured to poll the directory agent for updates of interest using `getAttributeValue()`. In two-party mode, the client may be configured to directly poll service agents. Like Jini and UPnP, service-variable monitoring may be used to monitor service descriptions. Also like Jini and unlike UPnP, the SLP service description has no associated TTL. The client can learn of service unavailability through non-responses to polls, which indicate the service has failed, or through unsuccessful attempts to use the service.

6.4 Web Services Discovery. The Web Services discovery (WS-Discovery) specification assumes, as a default, a two-party architecture in which clients rely on lazy and aggressive discovery to find service proxies, which advertise services. We assume two SDEs: a ServiceProxy SDE that acts on behalf of a service proxy and a Client SDE that acts on behalf of a client. Optionally, WS-Discovery supports the use of *Discovery Proxies* that act as gateways to external service discovery systems that use protocols other than WS-Discovery. If a Discovery Proxy announces its availability, a client employs it as an intermediary to discover services. If proxies are unavailable, the client reverts to the default two-party model. In addition, WS-Discovery supports complex service descriptions and administrative scopes. In Figure 6-5, we use our model to represent WS-Discovery in the default two-party architecture without Discovery Proxies. The blue boxes are classes we added to accommodate WS-Discovery. As we explain below, our model can also represent WS-Discovery with Discovery Proxies.

6.4.1 WS-Discovery without Discovery Proxies. In default mode, WS clients discover service proxies through lazy or aggressive discovery. The ServiceProxy SDE implements the advertiser role (shown in Figure 6-5 through the UML *implements* relationship to the class `Advertiser`) that acts on behalf of a `ServiceDescription`. The Client SDE implements the service seeker role (as represented by the implements relationships with the classes `ServiceSeeker` and `SeekerProxy`). Upon start-up, the service proxy invokes the advertiser's local announce operation, which sends a single multicast Hello message that corresponds to `ServiceProxy.lazyAnnouncement()`. WS-Discovery does not provide an algorithm for repeating announcements; therefore, we omit information about announcement cycle. To prevent message storms upon system restart (or associated with other synchronized behaviors), WS-Discovery requires announcements to be issued only after a random delay, distributed uniformly up to 500 s.

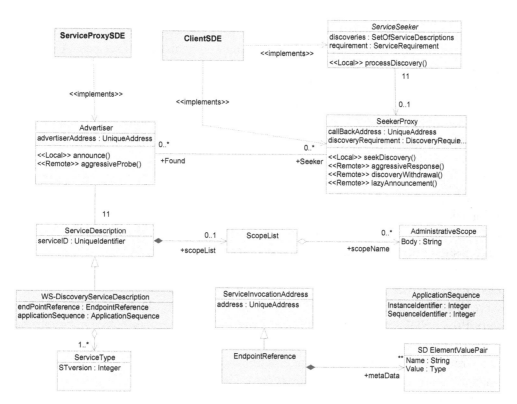

Figure 6-5. Class Diagram for WS-Discovery – yellow (or light gray) Classes taken from our Model; blue (or dark gray) Classes Required for WS-Discovery

The announcement carries a service description that we represent as a subclass, `WS-DiscoveryServiceDescription`. This specialized WS service description inherits (from the service description in our model) a globally unique service ID and a list of administrative scopes. The WS service description refines our concept of sequence number to the more complex formulation required by WS-Discovery, which contains: (1) an instance identifier that is incremented if the related service has failed, lost state, and restarted, (2) a sequence identifier that is unique in the context of a particular instance identifier, and (3) a message number. The version number in the service description included in our model could represent the WS-Discovery sequence identifier. We to represent the WS-Discovery message number as a parameter for the announcement, which is incremented each time an announcement occurs. The WS service description also replaces the service invocation address from our model with a WS endpoint reference (EPR), which includes metadata required to establish communications with the described service. In addition, the WS service description permits a service to have a list of service type names (rather than the single service type provided in our model). WS-Discovery permits dynamic changes to the EPR metadata, which must be followed by an announcement to disseminate the update. WS-Discovery also supports a multicast discovery withdrawal message, sent by the advertiser.

WS-Discovery supports an aggressive discovery procedure where a client can issue two types of multicast messages: *probe* and *resolve*. A probe message corresponds to a call to `Advertiser.aggressiveProbe()`, but with a discovery requirement that specifies a combination of desired service types and administrative scopes. A resolve message corresponds to a multicast aggressive probe with a discovery requirement that specifies a service ID. This implies WS-Discovery might require two steps in aggressive discovery: (1) find the service IDs for a set of services with desired types within desired administrative scopes and (2) find the service description associated with a particular service ID. Our model directly supports such two-step operations, which are similar to those required in UPnP. Aggressive probes that match service descriptions are followed by a unicast aggressive response message from the advertiser, represented in our model by invoking `SeekerProxy.aggressiveResponse()`, which conveys the service description (described above). WS-Discovery does not specify the use of repeated aggressive probes; therefore we omit any related parameters. Responses to aggressive probes are issued only after a uniformly distributed random delay.

6.4.2 Discovery Proxies. When deployed, Discovery Proxies participate in both lazy and aggressive discovery as described above. We would represent Discovery Proxies as a Discovery Proxy SDE (not shown) that implements the advertiser role. Discovery proxy advertisers distinguish themselves from regular service proxy advertisers by including a "discovery proxy" type in their announcements and aggressive probe responses (presumably as part of the list of service types). Upon receipt, the client is expected to initiate communications with the discovery proxy using a proxy-specific protocol, which is assumed to be the service discovery protocol with which the proxy is associated. Thereafter, the dialogue is specific to this discovery protocol. We assume that the client could switch to a different Client SDE that implements a seeker role that is specific to the service discovery protocols being used.

6.5 Globus Monitoring and Directory Service. The Globus Monitoring and Discovery Service (or Globus MDS) is a hierarchical directory system that allows service proxies to register information in directories. This information can include service descriptions, service variable values, and information about computing resources. Clients search directories to discover services and computing resources that fulfill their requirements, and then engage these resources to execute grid applications. A key feature of MDS is the ability to dynamically create an index of aggregated service description information, including service variable information, for all services and resources registered on directories within a hierarchy. This index enables higher-level, or *parent*, directories to aggregate and display generalized information about groups of resources that are registered with lower level, or *child*, directories. References in parent directories to resource entries in child directories allow more detailed information to be obtained. The leaf nodes of the tree comprise service proxies that contain the most specific information about individual services and resources. This provides clients with the ability to first query for generalized descriptions and then to make further requests for specific information. Requests for detailed information propagate through the hierarchy to leaf nodes, which return replies back through the hierarchy to the client. A client may, however, directly query a service proxy for which a reference is known. In what follows, we illustrate how our model can be used to represent several Globus MDS functions:

repository discovery, service registration, and service discovery (through service retrieval). We assume three SDEs: a DirectorySDE that acts on behalf of the directory, together with Service Proxy and Client SDEs that act on behalf of service proxies and clients, respectively.

6.5.1 Repository Discovery. Globus MDS employs a three-party service discovery architecture in which clients and service proxies discover directories in a straightforward way using a simplified version of directed discovery. Globus does not support aggressive or lazy discovery, though the specification states that other service discovery protocols may be used by a Globus system to supplement discovery. Globus does not explicitly support administrative scopes for repositories, though its hierarchical indexing system can be used to partition a namespace to achieve a similar result.

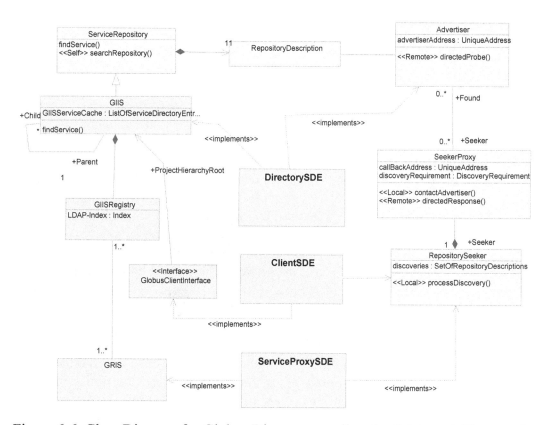

Figure 6-6. Class Diagram for Globus Discovery –yellow (or light gray) Classes taken from our Model; blue (or dark gray) Classes required for Globus MDS

The Globus service directory is known as the Grid Index Information Service (GIIS). To model this, the Directory SDE implements the repository and registry roles, represented in Figure 6-6 through the UML implements relationship to the class `GIIS`, whose superclass is `ServiceRepository`. The Globus GIIS contains a service registry and index-construction services, represented in our model by the class `GIISRegistry`. The behavior of the GIIS is described further below. The Directory SDE also implements the repository advertiser role, represented by the implements relationship to the class

`Advertiser`, which accepts directed probes from service proxies and clients. The advertiser acts on behalf of a simple repository description consisting of the address of the GIIS. Both the Client and ServiceProxy SDEs are pre-configured with the address of GIIS SDE directories to contact. In Figure 6-6, the Client SDE and ServiceProxy SDE both implement the role of repository seeker, represented using UML implements relationships to `RepositorySeeker` and `SeekerProxy`. This enables transmission (upon start-up) of a directed probe to a designated directory, which if received would be followed by a directed response indicating availability of the related GIIS.

For clients, the directory serves as an entry point, or *project root directory*, where queries are submitted to the MDS hierarchy through a `GlobusClientInterface`. The ServiceProxy SDE implements a Grid Resource Information Service (GRIS), represented by the class `GRIS`, to receive queries about resources it manages. Each GRIS may represent a large number of specific resources. Both client and service proxies may be given multiple directories to contact; thus a client may have multiple project root directories, while a service proxy may register with more than one GIIS. We note that the Globus procedure for contacting a GIIS does not specify sending repeated directed probes, nor describe actions to be taken if the directory cannot be located.

6.5.2 Service Registration and Extension. As shown in Figure 6-7, a Globus Directory SDE implements a Grid Index Information Service (GIIS), which can aggregate information from (both local and remote) GIIS registries. We represent a GIIS registry as a specialization of a service registry from our model. The service registry accepts registrations and also allows registered service descriptions to be changed. The GIIS registry specialization of service registry provides support for the Lightweight Directory Access Protocol (LDAP), which can be used to construct and maintain indices.

To register a service description, the ServiceProxy SDE implements the registration requestor role, through an indirect route, as shown in Figure 6-7, by implementing the class `GRIS`, which contains the `MdsRegistrationRequester` (a subclass of `ServiceRegistrationRequester`). As shown in Figure 6-7, a Globus Directory SDE may also implement the registration requester role, in order to propagate registrations to other directories in the MDS hierarchical directory. (The MDS requires child directories to propagate registrations with related service description information to the immediate parent GIIS.) Upon registration, the related service description and variable information is cached as a MDS *directory service entry*, represented by the class `ServiceDirectoryEntry`, and the GIIS index is updated accordingly. At higher levels in the MDS hierarchy, directory service entries are summarized to aggregate information about multiple resources. The summarization feature of MDS implies that information searchers might be required to seek more specific information from lower level directories. In our Globus model, both the Directory SDE and the ServiceProxy SDE can also request registration extensions by implementing the `ExtensionRequester` interface.

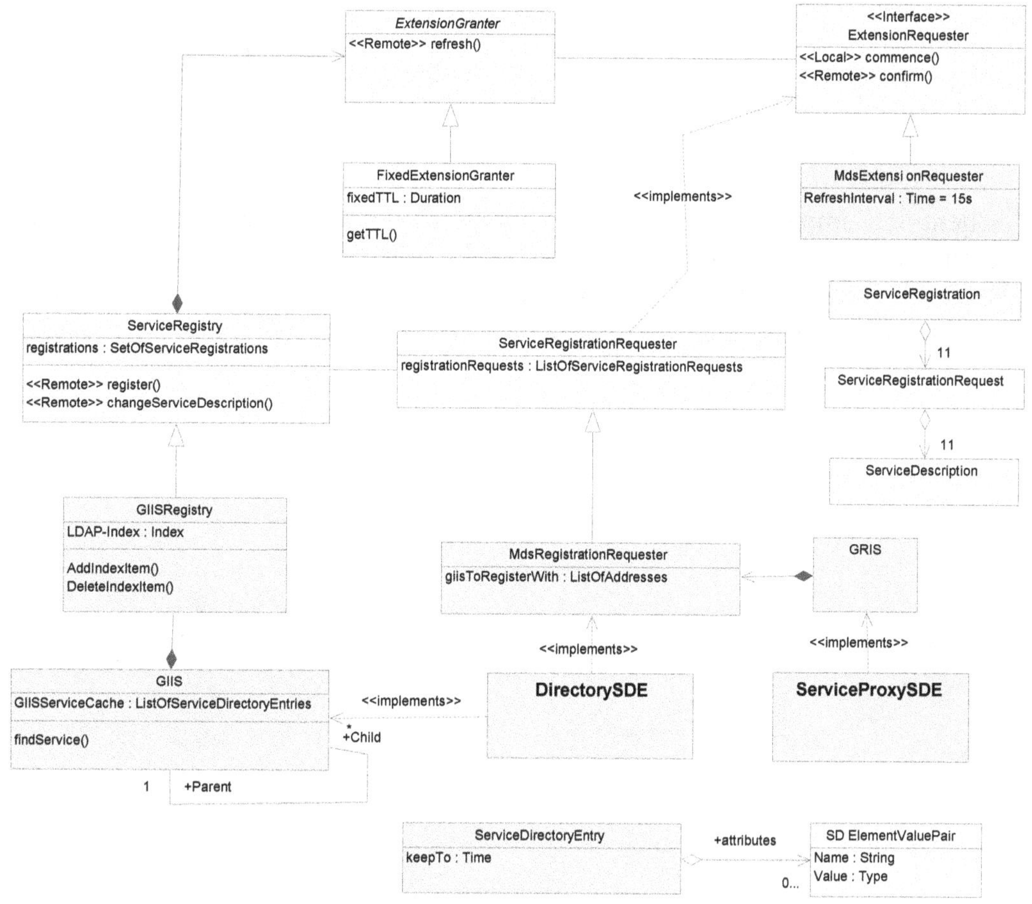

Figure 6-7. Class Diagram for Globus Service Registration

To accept registration requests for a service description, the Directory SDE inherits the `Registry.register()` operation. In Globus, registration requests do not specify a requested duration; instead, all registries in a Globus directory hierarchy are pre-configured to grant a constant duration (15 s by default). These traits are represented in Figure 6-7, where the Directory SDE implements a GIIS and related GIIS registry, which specializes a `ServiceRegistry` that includes a `FixedExtensionGranter` (specialization of `ExtensionGranter`). Globus supports periodic registration extension through a fixed-assignment strategy. A Globus registry will not purge a registration until two extension periods past without an extension request (i.e., Globus supports a default registration TTL of 30 s). Further, a Globus registry need not purge a registration that is subject of an on-going query (see 6.5.3).

6.5.3 Service Description Retrieval. Once registries have been discovered and services registered, Globus allows interested parties to search registries to retrieve service descriptions. Recall that in Globus several parties might wish to retrieve service descriptions. First, clients (Client SDE) wishing to find and use services may query for service descriptions. Second, Globus registries (Directory SDE) may need to query lower level registries to obtain summaries of service descriptions to reflect up the Globus registry hierarchy or to obtain detailed information to recursively answer a query. Third, a Globus service proxy (ServiceProxy SDE) may receive queries that require search of lower-level service components represented by the proxy. In this case, the proxy may need to query the lower level components. All three forms of service description retrieval are represented in Figure 6-8.

A Client SDE implements the role of a unicast service seeker, which allows the client to submit queries to an assigned "root directory" within the Globus directory hierarchy. Thus, each Globus client issues Globus queries (`grid-info-search`) to the GIIS of an assigned home directory. We model such queries as `GIIS.findService()`, a

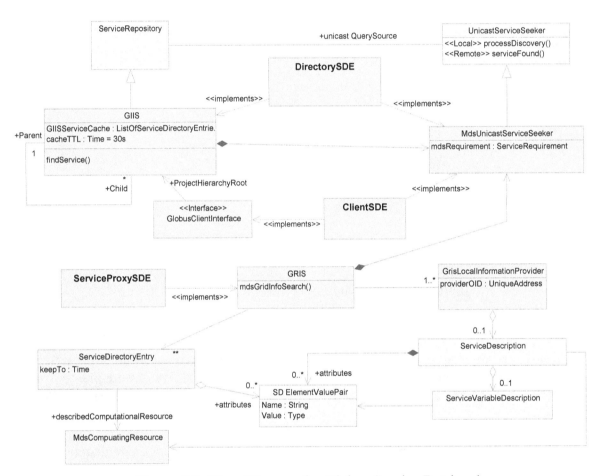

Figure 6-8. Class Diagram for Globus Service Retrieval

specialization of `ServiceRepository.findService()`, which includes: a list of attributes against which to match service description attributes and service variables, a maximum number of matches to return, and some Globus-specific parameters, such as the maximum number of directory hierarchy levels to traverse. Globus queries return only the location of matching services; to obtain more detail about a service, a client may be required to submit subsequent queries to traverse additional levels in the hierarchy or may be required to query a Service Proxy GRIS.

Each leaf-level GRIS has beneath it a number of local information providers (represented as the class `GrisLocalInformationProvider` in Figure 6-8) that handle requests for information about specific resources (such as processors, memory, and complex devices) that the GRIS service proxy advertises to the Globus directory hierarchy. We model each local information provider as a proxy for an individual resource, where the proxy has access to a detailed service description specific to the related resource. Modeled in this way, a GRIS may receive a query that must be decomposed into requests for information from local providers. The GRIS then must assemble the individual responses and forward an aggregate response to the query issuer, which is typically a GIIS seeking to obtain information to store as service directory entries that describe the attributes and variables associated with a set of available resources. Once deposited in some GIIS, service directory entries can be obtain by another GIIS and spread throughout a Globus directory hierarchy, becoming progressively more condensed and aggregated at higher levels.

When a GIIS receives a query it cannot match, the GIIS propagates the request to (child) GIIS directories at the next lower level (unless a query has traversed its maximum number of levels). We model this process (in Figure 6-8) by allowing a Directory SDE to implement the role of unicast service seeker. In Globus, service description information propagated upwards as part of a query response is stored temporarily ($keepTo$, default is 30 s) as a service directory entry in a local GIIS service cache.

7. Conclusions

Based on analyses of selected specifications for a first generation of service discovery systems, we were able to develop a generic model that unified the concepts, structure, and behavior encompassed in the various designs proposed by industry. Not only can our generic model represent all of the specific designs that we analyzed in creating the model, but also we demonstrated that our generic model could represent two service discovery designs we did not analyze during the creation of our model. Our generic model codifies and distinguishes fundamental concepts in the domain of service discovery systems, which enables analysis and comparison of specific designs based on the neutral terminology we created. As far as we know, our work provides the first domain model for service discovery systems. We suspect our generic model could provide a point of departure for vendor-neutral discussions about the possibility of standardizing service discovery architectures and protocols.

In the process of creating our model, we uncovered some limitations and open issues that exist with proposed designs for the first generation of service discovery systems. We suspect that our discussion of these issues may help potential users to understand the limits of applicability of current designs and may also help designers to improve the next generation of service discovery systems. Along these lines, we were able to identify three areas where current designs could exhibit limited performance when deployed at large scale. Further, we proposed various mechanisms that might be used to extend system performance and we discussed the ramification of adopting each mechanism. We suspect that this discussion could help implementers of service discovery systems to include mechanisms to improve the scalability and performance of first-generation service discovery systems.

In conducting our analysis, we noted that all designs for first-generation service discovery systems were silent with respect to service guarantees or goals that the designs aimed to achieve. To address this notable omission, we conceived service guarantees that we believe discovery systems should seek to satisfy. We also discussed various reasons why discovery systems might be unable to satisfy our proposed service guarantees. We represented our service guarantees in the context of our model and we formalized the guarantees as consistency conditions that service discovery systems should strive to maintain. We explained how we have applied our consistency conditions to evaluate the performance and correctness of designs for specific service discovery systems.

8. References

[1] Arnold K. et al. The Jini Specification, V1.0 Addison-Wesley 1999. The latest version is available on the Web from Sun Microsystems.

[2] Bieber G. and Carpenter J. "Openwings A Service-Oriented Component Architecture for Self-Forming, Self-Healing, Network-Centric Systems," from the web site: http://www.openwings.org/.

[3] Guttman E., Perkins C., Veizades J., and Day M. *Service Location Protocol*, V.2, Internet Engineering Task Force (IETF), RFC 2608, June 1999. The latest version is available on the IETF RFC web site.

[4] Kempf J. and St. Pierre P. Service Location Protocol for Enterprise Networks. Wiley and Son, Inc. (ISBN # 0-47-3158-7)

[5] Universal Plug and Play Device Architecture, V. 1.0, Microsoft, June 8, 2000. The latest version is available from the UPnP Forum web site.

[6] Specification of the Home Audio/Video Interoperability (HAVi) Archiecture, V1.1, HAVi, Inc., May 15, 2001. The latest version is available from the HAVi web site.

[7] Specification of the Bluetooth System, Core, Vol. 1, Version 1.1, the Bluetooth SIG, Inc., February 22, 2001, 1999. The latest version is available from the Bluetooth Consortium web site.

[8] Salutation Architecture Specification, V. 2.0c, Salutation Consortium, June 1, 1999. The latest version is available on the Salutation Consortium web site.

[9] Beatty J. et al. Web Services Dynamic Discovery (WS-Discovery) specification, February 2004. The latest version can be downloaded from the Web.

[10] The Globus Monitoring and Discovery Service. The latest information should be available on the Web. Here is one location: http://www-unix.globus.org/toolkit/mds/

[11] UDDI Version 3.0, Published Specification, Dated 19 July 2002. The latest version should be available from the OASIS web site.

[12] Richard G. "Service Advertisement and Discovery: Enabling Universal Device Cooperation," *IEEE Internet Computing*, September-October 2000, pp. 18-26.

[13] Pascoe B. "Salutation Architectures and the newly defined service discovery protocols from Microsoft and Sun: How does the Salutation Architecture stack up," Salutation Consortium whitepaper, June 6, 1999.

[14] Rekesh J. UPnP, Jini and Salutation - A look at some popular coordination frameworks for future network devices, Technical Report, California Software Lab, 1999. Available online from http://www.cswl.com/whiteppr/tech/upnp.html.

[15] Bettstetter C. and Renner C. "A Comparison of Service Discovery Protocols and Implementation of the Service Location Protocol", *Proceedings of the Sixth EUNICE Open European Summer School: Innovative Internet Applications*, EUNICE 2000, Twente, Netherlands, September, 13-15, 2000.

[16] Miller B. and Pascoe R. Mapping Salutation Architecture APIs to Bluetooth Service Discovery Layer, Version 1.0, Bluetooth SIG White paper, July 1, 1999.

[17] Dabrowski C. and Mills K. "Analyzing Properties and Behavior of Service Discovery Protocols using an Architecture-based Approach," in the *Proceedings of Working Conference on Complex and Dynamic Systems Architecture*, DARPA-sponsored, December 2001.

[18] Dabrowski C., Mills K., and Elder J. "Understanding Consistency Maintenance in Service Discovery Architectures during Communication Failure" in the *Proceedings of the 3rd International Workshop on Software Performance*, ACM, July 2002, pp. 168-178.

[19] Dabrowski C., Mills K., and Elder J. "Understanding Consistency Maintenance in Service Discovery Architectures in Response to Message Loss", in the *Proceedings of the 4th International Workshop on Active Middleware Services*, IEEE Computer Society, July 2002, pp. 51-60.

[20] Dabrowski C. and Mills K. "Understanding Self-healing in Service Discovery Systems" in the *Proceedings of the First ACM SigSoft Workshop on Self-healing Systems* (WOSS '02), November 18-19, 2002, Charleston, South Carolina, ACM Press, pp. 15-20.

[21] Dabrowski C., Mills K., and Rukhin A. "Performance of Service Discovery Architectures In Response to Node Failure," in the *Proceedings of the International Conference on Software Engineering Research and Practice* (SERP'03), CSREA Press June 23-26, 2003, pp. 95-101.

[22] Mills K. and Dabrowski C. "Adaptive Jitter Control for UPnP M-Search", in the *Proceedings of ICC 2003*, May 11-15, 2003 in Anchorage, Alaska.

[23] Mills K., Rose S., Quirolgico S., Britton M., and Tan C. "An Autonomic Failure-Detection Algorithm" in the *Proceedings of the 4th International Workshop on Software Performance* (WoSP 2004), January 14-16, 2004, San Francisco, California, ACM Press, p. 79.

[24] Tan C. and Mills K. "Performance Characterization of Decentralized Algorithms for Replica Selection in Distributed Object Systems". This paper has not yet been submitted for publication; however, a copy may be obtained from kmills@nist.gov.

[25] Manna Z. and Pneuli A. The Temporal Logic of Reactive and Concurrent Systems Specification. Springer-Verlag, New York, 1992.

[26] Rumbaugh J., Jacobson I., and Booch G. The Unified Modeling Language Reference Manual. Addison-Wesley, Reading, Mass., 1999. The latest version of the UML specification can be obtained from http://www.uml.org/.

[27] Czerwinski S.E. et al. "An Architecture for a Secure Service Discovery Service, Proceedings of the *Fifth Annual International Conference on Mobile Computing and Networks* (MobiCom '99), ACM, August 1999, pp. 24-35.

[28] Castro M. et al. "One Ring to Rule them All: Service Discovery and Binding in Structured Peer-to-Peer Overlay Networks", *The Proceedings of the Tenth ACM SIGOPS European Workshop*, ACM, September 22-25, 2002, Saint-Émilion, France.

[29] Verma D. C. et al. "SRIRAM: A scalable resilient autonomic mesh", *IBM SYSTEMS JOURNAL*, VOL 42, NO 1, 2003, pp. 19-28.

[30] Hsiao H-C and King C-T. "Neuron – A Wide-Area Service Discovery Infrastructure", *Proceedings of the International Conference on Parallel Processing* (ICPP '02), August 18-21, 2002, p. 455.

[31] Halepovic E. and Deters R. "JXTA Performance Model", draft submitted paper from the Department of Computer Science at the University of Saskatchewan. http://bistrica.usask.ca/madmuc/Grads/Emir/pub/Halepovic_JXTAPerformanceModel-Submitted.pdf

[32] Joseph S. "NeuroGrid: Semantically Routing Queries in Peer-to-Peer Networks", *Proceedings of the 1st International Workshop on Peer-to-Peer Systems* (IPTPS'02), March 7-8, 2002.

[33] Sundramoorthy V. et al. "Service discovery with FRODO", in *Proceedings of the 12th IEEE International Conference on Network Protocols* (ICNP), Berlin, Germany, October 2004, pp. 24-27.

[34] Sundramoorthy V. et al., "Functional principles of registry-based service discovery", in *Proceedings of the 30th IEEE Conference on Local Computer Networks* (LCN), Sydney, Australia, to appear in November 2005.

Appendix A. Function Sets, Functions, Roles, Mandatory Classes, and Role Operations

Discovery Function Set

Function	Role	Mandatory classes	Operations between roles
Aggressive Discovery	*Advertiser*	Advertiser, DiscoverableItem*	Advertiser.aggressiveProbe()
	Seeker	Seeker*, SeekerProxy, DiscoveryRequirement*	SeekerProxy.aggressiveResponse()
Lazy Discovery	*Advertiser*	Advertiser, DiscoverableItem	
	Seeker	Seeker*, SeekerProxy, DiscoveryRequirement*	SeekerProxy.lazyAnnounce()
Directed Discovery	*Advertiser*	Advertiser, DiscoverableItem	Advertiser.directedProbe()
	Seeker	Seeker*, SeekerProxy, DiscoveryRequirement*	SeekerProxy.directedResponse()
Discovery Withdrawal	*Advertiser*	Advertiser, DiscoverableItem	
	Seeker	Seeker*, SeekerProxy, DiscoveryRequirement*	SeekerProxy.discoveryWithdrawal()

Service Retrieval Function Set

Function	Role	Mandatory classes	Operations between roles
Service Search	*Repository*	ServiceRepository, ServiceDescription	ServiceRepository.findService()
	Service Seeker	UnicastServiceSeeker, ServiceRequirement	ServiceSeeker.serviceFound()
Attribute Query	*Repository*	ServiceRepository, ServiceDescription	ServiceRepository.findService() (with attribute selection)
	Service Seeker	UnicastServiceSeeker, ServiceDescription	ServiceSeeker.serviceFound()

Registration Function Set

Function	Role	Mandatory classes	Operations between roles
Registration (generic)	*Registry*	Registry, Registration	Registry.register()
	Registration Requester	Registration Requester	RegistrationRequester.[addConfirmed(), addDenied()]
Registration Cancellation	*Cancellation Requester*	RegistrationRequester	ExtensionRequester.cancel()
Service Registration	*Service Registry*	ServiceRegistry, ServiceRegistration, ServiceDescription	ServiceRegistry.register()
	Service Registration Requester	ServiceRegistration Requester, ServiceDescription	ServiceRegistrationRequester.[addConfirmed(), addDenied()]
Change Service	*Service Registry*	ServiceRegistry, ServiceRegistration	ServiceRegistry.changeService Description()
	Change Requester	ServiceRegistration Requester, ServiceDescription	ServiceRegistrationRequester.[changeConfirmed(),changeDenied()]
Notification Request Registration	*Full Registry*	FullRegistry, Notification Registration	FullRegistry.register()
	Notification Registration Requester	Notification Registration Requester, NotificationScope	NotificationRegistrationRequester.[addConfirmed(), addDenied()]
Notification	*Notification Provider*	FullRegistry, Notification	
	Notification Receiver	NotificationReceiver	NotificationReceiver.notification()
Event Registration	*VariableEvent Registry*	VariableEvent Registry	VariableEventRegistry.Register()
	Event Registration Requester	EventRegistration Requester	EventRegistrationRequester.[confirmed(), denied()]
Event Notification	*Event Provider*	EventableVariables, EventNotice	
	Event Receiver	EventReceiver	EventReceiver.eventNotice()
	Registry	Registry	

Registration Extension Function Set

Function	Role	Mandatory classes	Operations between roles
Registration Extension (refresh)	Extension Requester	ExtensionRequester, [Service,Notification] Registration	ExtensionRequester.Refresh()
	Extension Granter	*ExtensionGranter*, [Service,Notification] *Registration*	ExtensionGranter.[confirmed(), refreshDenied

Service Variable Monitoring			
Function	**Role**	**Mandatory classes**	**Operations between roles**
Get Monitorable Variables	*Variable Provider*	VariableProvider, ServiceVariable Description	VariableProvider. GetMonitorableVariables()
	Variable Accessor	VariableAccessor	VariableAccessor. monitorableVariablesFound()
Get Variable Information	*Variable Provider*	VariableProvider, ServiceVariable Description	VariableProvider. getVariableValues()
	Variable Accessor	VariableAccessor	VariableAccessor. variableValuesFound()

www.ingramcontent.com/pod-product-compliance
Lightning Source LLC
Chambersburg PA
CBHW080555060326
40689CB00021B/4868